CARLO GOLDONI

WORLD DRAMATISTS
In the same series:

WORLD DRAMATISTS

CARLO
OLDONI

HEINZ RIEDT

Translated by Ursule Molinaro

WITH HALFTONE ILLUSTRATIONS

FREDERICK UNGAR PUBLISHING CO.

NEW YORK

Translated, and adapted, from the original German. Published by arrangement with Friedrich Verlag, Velber, Germany

Copyright © 1974 by Frederick Ungar Publishing Co., Inc.
Printed in the United States of America
Library of Congress Catalog Card Number: 73-85411
Designed by Edith Fowler
ISBN: 0-8044-2729-1

CONTENTS

CHRONOLOGY

1707   25 February, Carlo Goldoni is born in the San Tomà section of Venice, in the fine-looking house that is now the Casa Goldoni, the International Center for Goldoni Research. Carlo's family belongs to the upper echelons of what Venetians still call "the common people," some of whom are about to evolve into the middle class. His grandfather, Carlo Alessandro, a native of Modena, is notary-magistrate for trade and commerce in the Republic of Venice. His father, Giulio, is an easy-going man who maintains his carefree outlook on life even when he is finally obliged to choose a profession. (Carlo Alessandro's estate had considerably dwindled by the time of his death.)

1712   Giulio Goldoni goes to Rome to study medicine. His wife, Margherita, is left behind in Venice, with the five-year-old Carlo and with Giampaolo, who is not quite three.

1719   Carlo studies grammar and rhetoric at the

For the convenience of the reader, all play titles are provided in English. Please see bibliography for Italian titles and translation data.

I

Jesuit College in Perugia, where his father temporarily settles after completion of his medical studies.

1720   Carlo studies philosophy at the Dominican College in Rímini.

1721–25   Carlo runs away with Florindo d'Maccheroni, when he embarks for Chiozza with his troop of comedians after a guest performance in Rímini. Carlo's father, who is currently practicing in Chiozza, takes him along when he visits his patients. Then Carlo is dispatched to Venice to his Uncle Indric, a lawyer, in whose office he is supposed to prepare for future studies of jurisprudence.

Carlo finds a million excuses to escape the writing desk and run off to the theater. Even during office hours he manages to sketch scenes and subjects for comedies. (He describes this in his foreword to the Pasquali edition of his *Memoirs*, his so-called Italian *Memoirs*.) But he submits to having his hair tonsured and enters the Ghislieri Divinity College in Pavia, where he has been given a scholarship. He attends lectures in jurisprudence at the local university. His free time is occupied with dramatic literature.

1725–26   He composes an *atellana*, a satire about the girls of Pavia, and offends several leading families. Goldoni can no longer remain at the Divinity College and returns to Chiozza Again his father forgives him and takes him along on visits to his patients.

With his father, Carlo travels as far as Udine and Gorizia. Some of his poems are printed in Udine. They are singular among his works for having a religious character.

1727   Continues study of jurisprudence in Modena. Carlo is so deeply affected by the torture to which a sinful monk is subjected in that city that he wants to enter a monastery in a fit of depression. But his father knows him better. A few visits to the theater, and the crisis is overcome.

1728 He becomes a magistrate in the court in Chiozza and later takes a higher post in Feltre.

1729 In Feltre he writes two intermezzi (short skits that were often performed between acts at that time).

1731 His father dies suddenly. In the fall, Carlo obtains his doctorate from the University of Padua.

1732 He is admitted to the bar in his native Venice.

1733 Goldoni brilliantly wins his first case, but is forced to flee the city in order to escape financial pressures and a totally unwelcome marriage. A destitute traveler, he passes through Vicenza, Verona, Brescia, and Bergamo, and finally arrives in Milan with hopes for a successful production of his musical drama, *Amalasunta*. But the play is rejected. In his disappointment Goldoni throws the manuscript into the fireplace.

He becomes chamberlain to the ambassador of the Republic of Venice, whom he accompanies to Crema in the course of the turmoils of war. In Crema he is promoted to secretary. A year later, disagreements crop up between the two, and Goldoni moves on. On the walls of Parma he witnesses a real battle. In Casalpusterlengo he is robbed of all his belongings. Via Brescia he travels to Verona, where he meets the director of the Teatro San Samuele in Venice, Giuseppe Imer. He returns to Venice as Imer's guest.

1734 His historical tragedy *Belisario* is a great success at the Teatro San Samuele. The owner of the theater, a nobleman by the name of Michele Grimani, entrusts Goldoni with the direction of his second theater, the Teatro San Giovanni Crisostomo, for the years 1737 to 1741. According to the twentieth-century critic Manlio Dazzi, this first contact with the theater is still a "falling in love, an engagement rather than a marriage."

1736   Carlo Goldoni marries Nicoletta Connio, a lawyer's daughter from Genoa.

1738   Goldoni becomes involved in comedy-type theater for the first time when he writes the principal scenes of *A Man of the World* for Antonio Sacchi (well-known at that time by his stage name, Truffaldino), the brilliant Arlecchino.

1741–43   At the end of his contract with the Teatro San Giovanni Crisostomo, Goldoni becomes honorary consul of Genoa in Venice, a position to which he applies himself with more zeal than aptitude. It earns him no money but a great deal of experience with merchants.

1743   Antonio Sacchi has left the Teatro San Samuele. Goldoni writes *A Lady of Charm*, his first comedy with a complete text. He just has time to read it to the actors when, in the summer, he is again forced to leave Venice in order to escape the creditors of his brother Giampaolo. With his wife he travels in pursuit of the Duke of Modena, who still owes him money and who is, at this point, waging a war in the Romagna province.

1744–45   For the duration of the carnival season Goldoni assumes the direction of the theater in Rímini. He travels through Tuscany and finally settles in Pisa as a lawyer. Antonio Sacchi requests from him a scenario of *The Servant of Two Masters*, based on an older French theme. Goldoni complies.

1746–48   Sacchi is responsible for the play's world

premiere on <u>Milan</u>. (<u>The complete text is not to be written until 1753</u>.) Girolamo Medebac, the director of the Teatro Sant'Angelo in Venice, knows as well as Sacchi that Goldoni is born for the theater. Goldoni and Medebac reach an agreement. Goldoni renounces the financial security of the practice of jurisprudence and returns to Venice. This time, his return to the theater becomes a relationship for life. For the next five years (1748–53), Goldoni is Medebac's writer-in-residence at the Teatro Sant'Angelo. Thus begins the great period of theater reform implemented by Goldoni.

Goldoni's comedy *The Cunning Widow* is performed in 1748.

1749 *A Girl of Honor* is performed next. For the first time the common people are given equal importance on stage during the *gondolieri* scenes. All of Goldoni's characters are becoming more and more consciously the representatives of specific social levels (a process that began about 1747).

1749–50 *The Good Wife* and *The Gentleman and the Lady* are performed. The latter is the first Italian commedia without masks. Today, this play strikes us as completely harmless, but ten years after it was first performed, the nobility was still up in arms against Goldoni, who had "exposed the secrets of gallantry to the profane eyes of the rabble," as the Marchese Albergati complained to Voltaire in 1761. *The Antique Dealer's Family* is performed during this same season.

After a flop at the end of the season, Goldoni promises his public sixteen new comedies within the year. (His contract called "only" for eight.) He keeps his promise.

1750–51 Some of his most important plays are put on stage during this time. Among them is *The Funny Theater*, which contains the outline of his reform program, disguised as a comedy within a comedy. (Pirandello is later to use the same device, as Plautus had done centuries earlier.) Other plays are: *Women Are Touchy*, a play of social criticism that is almost indecent for its time; *The Coffeehouse*; *The Liar*; *Women's Gossip*.

In 1751 with Medebac he produces his first "sin" in Torino, an ambitious play entitled *Molière*, in fourteen-syllable so-called Martellian verse.

1752 He writes *The Wise Wife*, *The Jealous Women*, and *The Loving Servant Maid*, a mixture of touchiness, drama, and comic situations.

1753–56 His masterpiece, *Mirandolina: The Mistress of the Inn*, and *The Inquisitive Women* are performed (1753). These plays mark the highpoint and the finale of his collaboration with Medebac at the Teatro Sant'Angelo. He signs a three-year contract with the nobleman Vendramin for the Teatro San Luca, committing himself to produce eight comedies a year for six hundred ducats. But difficulties begin to accumulate. The actors must be won over to Goldoni's new subject matter and to the new style and form of his plays: the new theater reform was marked, in part, by the abolishing of masks and the introduction of texts that were written down in full by the author and were to be respected by the actors.

death of improv!

On top of that, a regular "theater war" breaks out between Goldoni and a literary adventurer by the name of Chiari, whom Medebac has hired. The "sins in rhyme" that are the result of this warfare are not worth mentioning. Still, among Goldoni's rhymed comedies are a number of delightful bits, such as *The Housewives* (1755), *Women at Home* (1755), and the charming *Campiello* (1756). All are written in Venetian dialect.

Vendramin renews Goldoni's contract for five more years: a minimum of six comedies a year for one hundred ducats each.

making a living as an artist

1757   Goldoni writes *The War*.

1760   *The Impresario from Smirna* and the two comedies that mark the beginning of his artistic liberation, *The Lovers* and *Gentlemen of the Old School*, are produced at the carnival.

1760–61   During this season, *A Curious Accident* and *The New House* deserve special mention.

1761–62   During this particularly fruitful season, Goldoni writes *Summer-vacation Mania*, *Summer-vacation Adventures*, and *The Return from Summer Vacation*. They are followed by *The Honorable Todero the Grouch* and *Much Ado in Chiozza*, one of Goldoni's best-constructed works and most important dramas. And finally his goodbye to Venice, *One of the Last Nights of the Carnival*.

1762   Goldoni accepts the invitation of the *comédie italienne* and goes to Paris. Ever since 1754, the year in which his mother died, Goldoni's health had been failing. He worries about what will become of him financially in his old age. (The Republic of Venice refuses to grant him a pension.) But most of all it is the antagonism of Carlo Gozzi that drives him away. Gozzi not only uses his *fiabe* (theatrical fairy tales) against him but even starts circulating rumors about Goldoni.

On the other hand, Voltaire had acknowledged Goldoni's genius a number of years before, and so Goldoni sets out for Paris, full of hopes. He makes preparations as though he were going on a pleasure trip. But his expectations are soon disappointed. He discovers that all serious theater remains the prerogative of the *comédie française*, whereas nothing but nonsense, clowning, and *arte*-type improvisations are expected of the *comédie italienne*. Goldoni has to resign himself to the situation. For two years he writes scenarios.

1765   In February he leaves the *comédie italienne*. Soon after he writes *The Fan*, which he sends to Venice. But being unable to live on such income, he becomes Italian instructor to Adélaïde, the daughter of Louis XV, and lives at Versailles.

1774   Goldoni starts writing his memoirs, *The Memoirs of Mr. Goldoni, for a Better Understanding of the History of His Life and of His Theater*, which are first published in a French edition (1787).

1775   Meanwhile he has become Italian instructor to Princess Elizabeth, sister of Louis XVI. (While Goldoni is instructing the ladies of France in Italian, Beaumarchais is teaching them how to play the harp and the guitar.)

1780   Goldoni has trouble with his eyes. He leaves Versailles and moves back to Paris. He is obliged to sell his entire beloved library to finance the move.

1792   The Royal Civil List, which had paid a small pension to Goldoni, is abolished. For seven months he lives in utter poverty.

1793   On 6 February the National Convention renews his pension, following the appeal of Marie-Joseph Chénier, who addresses the National Convention as follows:

"In the name of the Committee for Public

Education I wish to plead the cause of an aged foreigner, a writer of great excellence whose talent and greatness command the respect of all of Europe. Goldoni, an intelligent author and moralist whom Voltaire has called "Italy's Molière," was called to Paris in 1762 by the *ancien régime*. Since 1768 he has received a pension of 3600 livres a year. He has no other income. . . .

At this point, one of our decrees is condemning this octogenarian, who achieved such great merit in France as well as in Italy with his outstanding work, to a life of misery. Citizens . . . you will not refuse a helping hand to the noblest things on this earth, to virtue, to genius, and to misfortune."

6 or 7 February: Goldoni does not live to hear Chénier's words. Shortly before his eighty-sixth birthday he dies, poor and blind. His grave is unknown.

Goldoni's middle-class background gave him easy access to both the higher and the lower strata of society. But most of all it explained his understanding of and confidence in his own class, a confidence that runs through his entire work. His roaming all over Italy broadened his outlook, which was already wide because of having been exposed to a variety of situations and people since childhood. Accompanying his father on his medical visits, magisterial offices at the criminal courts, his legal practice—all this sharpened his analytical understanding and heightened his critical faculties, but did not in any way curtail the kindness of his heart or his generosity. (Echoes from the life of a lawyer can be sensed in a number of his comedies.)

All these factors helped him to discover *life*, and to transpose it for *theater* use into stage language and gestures. He had no other interests. His education was eclectic, his knowledge not particularly vast. His work is informed by his natural genius, by sensitive understanding, by a humanity based on the law of nature and on the ideas of the Enlightenment, by a special sense of social and family interrelatedness.

The totality of Goldoni's work comprises 5 tragedies, 16 tragicomedies, and 137 comedies, of which only the better-known have been mentioned in the above chronology. In addition he wrote 57 scenarios for the actors of the commedia dell'arte (also known as the *commedia a braccia*).

His 20 intermezzi for musical theater, 13 dramas, 55 libretti for song-plays and opera buffas, and 3 musical farces are almost forgotten today. Yet, Goldoni's initial recognition outside Italy was due to the musical productions of his works. Between 1754 and 1775 he composed 18 texts for the court theater in Dresden.

His most successful libretti include *The Country Philosopher*, set to music by Galuppi (performed in Dresden in 1755), and *The Good Girl*, set to music by Piccinni, the most frequently produced comic opera of the eighteenth century. Haydn wrote the music for *The World on the Moon* and *The Fisherwomen*. Mozart wrote the music for *A Simple Ruse*, as reworked by Coltellini. Vivaldi, Paisiello, and Salieri also wrote music for libretti by Goldoni.

The twentieth-century theater critic Giuseppe Ortolani wrote: "It would be easy to count fifty eighteenth-century composers who used libretti by Goldoni. His musical comedies gave composers greater freedom; contributed to more extensive orchestration; tied choruses in at the beginning, in the middle, and at the ending of acts; and combined male and female voices in tercets, quartets, and quintets in his happy and loud finales."

This enormous production (to which a number of lost manuscripts must certainly be added) is indicative of two factors: financial necessity and a wealth of artistic invention.

GOLDONI'S TIME AND WORK

"Three cities share in the glory of having given birth to comedy: Athens, Paris, and Venice," wrote Niccolò Tommaseo. It is to Goldoni that Venice owes this glorious repute. The Goldoni who said that the two books he never tired of reading were the *world* and the *theater*.

The world, to him, was basically and foremost Venice. A Venice whose position as a political power was already in full decline. A Venice that was no longer the mediator between Orient and Occident. That was rapidly falling behind France, England, and Holland, the upcoming commercial powers. A metropolis nonetheless, still hospitable and openminded, during this last century of a thousand years of freedom.

Eighteenth-century Venice had one hundred sixty printers. It was the century of the great musicians Antonio Lotti, Benedetto Marcello, Baldassare Galuppi (known as Buranello), Giuseppe Tartini, Antonio Vivaldi; of the painters Piazzetta and Tiepolo, of Rosalba Carriera and Alessandro Longhi, of Canaletto, of Francesco Guardi, and of Pietro Longhi.

But these were also the days of fermenting social

changes. High nobility was still maintaining the city-state in a remarkable equilibrium with the existing oligarchy. The orgies and loose morals that inspired so many romantic legends about Venice and precipitated its downfall had not yet begun. Still, nobility was becoming marketable. A number of bankrupt noblemen who had lost all but their titles were relegated to San Barbara, a section of the city that was forced to take them in, while state and church footed the bill. They were the leeches and informers, the parasites of society who made the people snicker. Goldoni snickered with the "people": the gondolieri and fishermen, waiters and grocers' wives, merchants and lacemakers, doctors and lawyers.

Merchants and intellectuals (as we would call them today) made up the more and more consciously forming middle class. They were not prerevolutionary as in France. They were industrious and had unshakable faith in their own future. All indications of a rising social class.

In music and the arts remarkable works were being put forth, inspired by the climate and reality of their time, but the theater was stagnant, although, as a mass medium, it should have been particularly dedicated to cultivating dialogue.

And it was not lagging behind its time either. It had stopped ages ago, on a long-abandoned road, and lost all direction. Though friends and relations may occasionally have topped its petrified features with a pious toupee, it could no longer catch up with its era.

The situation was the same all over Italy, not only on the many stages of Venice. Nevertheless the public still expected from the theater the type of entertainment that was eventually to be provided by the novel. The need for theatrical communication remained unbroken.

Meanwhile, Molière and the French theater had come to Italy. As a reaction, the Arcadia was founded in Rome in 1690, an eclectic academy of classical orientation that tried to model public taste according to the classical literary rules promulgated by Petrarca and Anachreon. From it was derived the *teatro erudito*, the intellectual theater that copied antiquity. It was the creation of a closed stratum of society, the aristocracy. Attempts at reform ended in nothing more than prescriptions of style and remained, therefore, without any effect. Yet, two centuries earlier Venice had offered realistic theater, plays by Andrea Calmo (ca. 1510–71) and especially by Beolco, which portrayed the common people with their woes and their schemes.

Angelo Beolco (ca. 1502–1542) was an Italian dramatist and actor, whose stage name was Il Ruzzante. In many ways Beolco's work strikes us as modern today. He debunked authority, expressed pacifist ideals, and condemned war. Moreover, his productions broke with the tradition of theatrical illusion and emotionality. His theater was the forerunner of the proletarian theater of the radical counterrevolution, a theater that did not survive the political upheavals. Only recently has Beolco's work been rediscovered, and we are learning to appreciate it again. In Goldoni's days it was of no importance whatsoever.

Of course Goldoni was still familiar with the commedia dell'arte (also known as the *commedia a braccia*), a mixture of body control and spontaneity that the literary historian Richard Alewyn called "a strange phenomenon, a fluid cross between the most abstract geometry and creatural exuberance." Born directly of the people, it was a native Italian theater that left many an important formal legacy to the new movement in the offing.

1. The Commedia dell'Arte

Goldoni's relationship, or lack of relationship, to this type of theater has often been completely misunderstood. A few words about the origins and characteristics of the commedia dell'arte might therefore be in order.

It started with minstrels and tightrope dancers who began appropriating a few *cavajoles*—spoofs about the dumb hicks from the little town of Cava, a kind of gag that already existed in Italian folklore. This was then amalgamated with similar material from southern and northern Italy. To this an occasional loan from Plautus or Terence was thrown in.

Basically it was a histrionic reaction to the mystery plays of the middle ages. From the very outset the commedia dell'arte had a strange twofold character, a mixture of artful rope dancing and market noise, of artistry and popular satire. The result was a body control of the utmost precision and of boundless primitive vitality. A potent mixture indeed.

Toward the end of the sixteenth century it took on its characteristic form. Then came the time of its flowering. Specific types had crystallized—masked figures of which only the best-known will be mentioned here—which were still in existence in Goldoni's day.

The Venetian merchant Pantalone with his long beard; the doctor of jurisprudence from Bologna with a silk mask; and the two servants Arlecchino and Brighella, with brown leather masks to indicate their peasant origins.

The young chambermaid was, of course, as indispensable as the conventionally banal pair of lovers. (Pedrolino was exported to France, where he had better luck than in Italy and became the sad-eyed

Pierrot. Later, much later, he returned as Pierrot to his Italian homeland.)

The stage consisted only of a small platform. The set was always the same: a street or a marketplace, with a housefront, and a workable window as an additional entry or exit.

Anything "happening" outside the visible scene was related in great detail. And this in itself should make us pause and wonder. Was this improvisational theater? A happening on the spur of the moment? Far from it. The all-pervading rule of the *arte* comedians was to give the appearance of total spontaneity, as though everything, including the *lazzi*—mimed declamatory spoofs and sorties—were being exchanged on the spur of the moment like so many multicolored balls.

Gradually there evolved a standard repertory of *lazzi* (the "fresh urine" *lazzo*, the "fruit and kisses" *lazzo*, the "fly" *lazzo*). These were performed within a fairly limited repertory of scenarios. (The audience was perfectly familiar with the basic action.) These were summary outlines of childishly primitive events, usually the development of some amorous adventure.

Rehearsing and embroidering were up to the director, and memory lapses were filled in by a prompter. But rehearsals were strict, and everything worked to perfection. Everything was handled with an art that is not seen at today's Punch and Judy shows or clowns' acts in the circus.

Pantomime and tricks are essential elements (inherited from the illusionists, the *saltimbanchi*). Each character has a definite behavior pattern. Arlecchino is clumsy and devious, a lewd glutton; he cannot possibly act in any other way. He also has an inalterable range of gestures. His bow or entering leap has been blocked to an inch, with precision legwork, and is completely distinct from that of a Brighella or a Pantalone. (The legacy from tightrope dancing.) Geared only for outside effect, but with an absolute, unique precision. Success was inevitable. Troops of these frolicking fanatics and precision maniacs delighted Catherine de Medicis, Henri IV, and Louis XIV with their tall tales and leaps. Amusing and surprising audiences in France, Spain, England, Russia, and Germany, they became a legend. Only Italy was more measured in its praise, since Italy knew what they were all about, and judged them more soberly, in spite of the Italian readiness to share a joke.

It would, moreover, be an error to read real-life situations and political implications into the brazenly dumb jokes and calculatedly abstract follies of the *arte* performances. (To interpret the role of the Capitano, actually a never completely successful type portrayal, as the "people's protest" against the Spanish occupation seems altogether too patriotic and ideological.)

Animal instincts and lust, as best portrayed by the Arlecchino, under whatever name or nuance, before, during, and after the artistic performance, make up the substance of the commedia dell'arte. Ethics did not enter into it.

As a reaction to the medieval mystery plays the commedia dell'arte remained in a certain sense a product of the middle ages. Its trivialties were already anachronistic when Raffael painted his madonnas. In Goldoni's time it had "played itself out," and had become stuck in mechanical standardization. The world was changing, and neither an Antonio Sacchini's brilliant Arlecchino-Truffaldino nor a Carlo Gozzi's stubborn determination could put the wheel of time in reverse.

The above does not mean to be a denial of the theatrical merits of the commedia dell'arte, merely of its retrospective overestimation.

The *figli dell'arte*, the *arte* comedians, were practically born on stage. Paradoxically, society's contempt for their status, a blatant injustice by today's standards, worked to the advantage of their art. Anyone who became a comedian for whatever reason could not exercise any other "honorable" profession for as long as he lived. In this way a tightly closed circle developed. Outcast from other artisans with stable family traditions, they practiced strict discipline and were bent solely on the perfection of their craft. The commedia dell'arte's unique technical contribution, its exuberant performances and popular appeal, amply suffice to reserve it an important place in the history of the theater. It needs no additional legend.

2. *Goldoni's Theater Reform*

The world and the theater were the two "books" Goldoni had not only "read" without "tiring" of them but also "used."

In other words, he did not treat the two as separate entities, nor did he adapt thoughtlessly. He learned from them, on the contrary, distilled them, established their interrelationship, and transformed the lyrical potential of the world into theater poetry.

This is the indispensable key to his theater, as well as to his personality as an artist. Goldoni was a difficult playwright, but one who must be approached with an open mind (simply and naturally, as he himself said), without prejudice. He cannot be catalogued, nor classified according to extraneous standards.

For this reason he was grossly misunderstood from the start, and critics and directors have tried to impose on him their own one-sided simplifications. Not until the International Goldoni Congress, which was held in

Venice in 1957, did he receive a pertinent historico-critical evaluation, while stage interpretations ranged from Simoni to Visconti to Strehler.

The world from which Goldoni worked, with which he felt familiar, and was related to as an artist, was Venice, without the slightest touch of provincialism. It was the Venice of brewing social changes and bourgeois self-affirmation. But Goldoni's art went further, became an overall phenomenon, a "problem" that touched all of Europe and finally culminated in a comprehensive "analysis of the human heart," a human interrelatedness as such, as which it returned to the Goldonian houses and streets "with many an additional grain of truth."

Experiments, insights, and setbacks lined the path toward Goldoni's full artistic unfolding, toward his inner and outer liberation. Some plays were written according to demand, out of financial necessity. (Royalties were not yet in existence; only fixed payments per work.) These are factors that a critical evaluation of his work must not overlook. I am referring to the flexibility of the external form, the development of his theater that reaches from the commedia dell'arte to bourgeois theater, to hints of romanticism, and even foreshadows the verismo of a Giovanni Verga. It is partially because of this that Goldoni is regarded as the rejuvenator of Italian comedy as well as the pioneer of the new Italian theater as such.

There is one external factor to keep in mind: professional actors did not exist in Goldoni's time. His work was performed by *arte* comedians who played everything, including tragedy. Goldoni's dialogue therefore had to be written with an eye on the limitations of the *arte* actors.

Initially, Goldini erected a monument for the commedia dell'arte with *The Servant of Two Masters*, which was written as a scenario for the mime Antonio

Sacchi. Goldoni later wrote it out in full, to avoid unsuitable extemporizations, a practice Goldoni was emphatically against.

Ideally if not subjectively, this play constitutes the crowning glory of the commedia dell'arte. It is only at this point that we might be tempted to agree with the critic Siegfried Melchinger's comment that Goldoni "rediscovered improvisation, the commedia's basic element, with a stupendous instinct, and reinterpreted it anew." This opinion would be accurate, had the origins of the commedia been satire whose roots were in reality, not a mixture of abstraction and vulgar buffoonery.

It is true the vivacious monument of *The Servant of Two Masters* contributed in a special way to keep the lovable character of Arlecchino alive beyond the *arte* days. Regrettably, however, the continued success of the play established a stereotype, one that has misled many people into thinking that they can judge the totality of Goldoni's theater. *The Servant of Two Masters* already contained the seed of something new rather than of something merely "reexpressed." What Goldoni was doing was misunderstood especially outside of Italy, but not by his Venetian contemporaries, whose eyes pierced the brown leather masks.

Giorgio Strehler, director of the Piccolo Teatro in Milan, who was recently awarded the Goethe Prize, drew the proper conclusions from his observation. His first production was succeeded by a more appropriate second, and a third. Through the brown leather masks, as through any mask Goldoni used, the human face can be seen. The cocoon that shrouds the "figure" becomes more and more unraveled. Face and character become more evident as Goldoni's comedy developed (in the fullest, widest sense of the word). This development led to a realistic character portrayal that may be qualified as psychological realism. This is why, according to critic and historian Ettore Caccia, Goldoni "began writing his parts out in full, in order to prevent an overly colorful, overly subjective interpretation. This, in turn, led to the dissolution of masked theater."

This is in no way changed by the fact that Goldoni consciously maintained certain stock characters of the commedia dell'arte, as well as type characterizations from other traditions, which he evolved and adapted in his sense.

Let us take a look at the characters of the Servant and of Pantalone. Whether he is called Arlecchino, Brighella, Fabrizio, or whatever—the Servant is becoming a thinking human being who represents a viewpoint considered revolutionary in his day, one Beaumarchais's Figaro was later to espouse: Only a worthy authority deserves obedience.

The second character, be he called Pantalone, or by any other "bourgeois" name, becomes a totally new Goldonian character, a Venetian merchant who is typical of the entire Venetian middle class. The "theatrical evolution" of this character can serve as a measure of Goldoni's own evolution, from rational optimism to arational faith in the power of the emotions, an evolution that reaches far beyond the scope one usually grants Goldoni.

Literary history does acknowledge that he expanded his characters, as for instance from the conventional chambermaid (Smeraldina) to the self-possessed burgher's daughter (Mirandolina). But in actuality his psychology goes much further, and foreshadows a sensitivity that does not come into its own before romanticism.

Most textbooks express the opinion that Goldoni's theater reform abolished the masks and substituted fully written texts for the scenarios. This renders only half the truth. Moreover it conveys the erroneous assumption that he merely continued and updated the commedia dell'arte (as though that had been the only kind of theater in existence). Masked-theater troupes continued to travel through Italy and abroad, and to perform in the "old tradition," and no other. There is little doubt that the demise of masked theater was due not directly to Goldoni. It was essentially a historical phenomenon that had nothing to do with him. Goldoni was neither the successor nor the destroyer of the commedia dell'arte.

3. Goldoni's View of Life

Comedy suited Goldini's nature; comedy in its widest sense, that is, according to the Italian distinction between *commedia* and *tragedia*. His comedies are neither farces nor the heavy-handed bourgeois entertainment of the nineteenth century. To a large extent they are "dramatized amusements," with equal emphasis on entertainment and on morality.

Elio Vittorini defined the Goldoni comedy very precisely:

> His comedy is comedy mainly in the sense of the "human comedy," not unlike Boccaccio's tales or Shakespeare's tragedies. Not being "divine" comedy, it does not view the human condition in its relation to a "higher absolute" from which it derives full significance. . . . He was not interested in lifting "a thing" out of the "insignificance" in which he found it, and giving it omnipotence in the romantic limitlessness of a realm that must be conquered. He wanted to show that "a thing" could be great within its own "smallness," precisely within the "minimal" dimension in which

popular tradition, theatrical convention, or plain common sense have placed it.

In other words, Goldoni restored the freedom of the theater. He ignored the sterile classicism of the Arcadia, with its coating of rationalism, as well as the commedia dell'arte, with its paralyzed patterns and its vulgarity. He wanted no part of old-fashioned forms, of anything that is alien to life. He discussed everyday reality with his audiences, who recognized themselves effortlessly, enthusiastically, in the prototypes he created for them. He spoke to people about people, in general terms but without being vague. He never portrayed detached abstractions. His characters were always "true to life." He aroused likes and dislikes and stimulated compassion in the Aristotelian sense.

Goldoni scholar Nicola Mangini pointed to the extensive "social attention" that Goldoni mobilized as he sifted the manifold expressions of everyday life. This led to his active crystallization of the three levels of society: (1) the decadent aristocracy, with its "condescending mannerisms," its pretentiousness ("What good are titles? Why all this vanity? Nothing but prejudices!"); (2) the aspiring middle class with which he felt at home, but criticized wherever necessary (he takes us into their houses, not into the luxury dwellings of the aristocracy); (3) the common people, whom he treated with affection—and as a valid partner, on stage as well as in life.

He did this at a time when rich noblemen in their boxes "thought nothing of spitting down on the mob in the orchestra," according to Goldoni's biographer, H. C. Chatfield-Taylor.

Goldoni was not engaged in ideologically determined polemics. Neither was he heralding a "protest of the people against the feudal lords," a "whole social program," as the Soviet scholar A. K. Dshivelegov would like to prove. But he was committed to his time. Artistically as well as humanly, he defended a moral code that he derived from the law of nature. Moreover, he shared Diderot's conviction that theater should be educational (a few grains of truth interspersed with the fun).

Of this aspect of Goldoni, literary critic Walter Binni wrote:

> Most of all he had a deep sense of the value of life, and fullest confidence in life's well-defined tangible limitations.
>
> Metaphysical and transcendental explanations and definitions did not exist for him. . . .
>
> He accepted the limits of reality (the social and political concepts of the reform in their most popular general expression) with confidence and good humor. He loved reality (especially the human reality of houses and cities, relationships between people, the solid ground on which the rich, fascinating adventure of life takes place). . . .
>
> Goldoni was a true poet of this vital point of view, filled with the deepest sympathy for people and objects.

Goldoni's commitment to life had no philosophical or doctrinaire overtones. He was positively an optimist. It is not surprising that the German romantics (in particular A. W. Schlegel) accused Goldoni of superficiality because he attempted to depict the totality of life by means of a multitude of everyday incidents. Nothing in his work allows for a "life within," whereas he gave loving attention to all the things that the romantics looked down upon, handling affectionately the reality of everyday banality that the romantics found restricting.

It was not until our era that this "superficiality" has finally found its meaning again. Pirandello wrote that the new theater was born "when this extraordinarily fresh expression of life burst upon the mummified Italian theater and restored its breath, warmth, and movement. . . ."

Goldoni's freshness and movement came not only from his relationship to life as such, but also from his very special way of handling his material dramatically. His many analytical observations of reality yield the desired synthesis only when he gathered them into a choruslike effect.

Faults and virtues of Goldoni's characters are not derived from coincidence or from a single overall problem. (Unlike Molière's characters, for instance.) The characters are, on the contrary, rooted in "normal" life, and always have a social significance since they all deal with human relationships in a narrow as well as in the larger sense.

This emphasis on community life is typically Latin, and its problems have a greater impact than the deep, searching inwardness that is the mainspring of writing north of the Alps.

Denis Diderot, Goldoni's contemporary, stressed social differences as one of the richest sources of dramatic conflicts for his *comédie sérieuse*. He wrote: "What a wealth of important detail; of public and private actions! What unknown truths, what new situations to be drawn from this well!"

"Public and private actions," "new situations," drawn from the study of social differences are food for the theater and automatically link it to society as its irreversible "mirror, a diary in a nutshell."

In the history of the theater Goldoni is unsurpassed for his portrayal of community life. His best scenes always have as many characters as he could legitimately draw in. He rarely wrote walk-on parts. His interest in life is rooted in the many aspects of human encounters, and therefore no person is superfluous.

Goldoni wrote: "Every character has his own characteristics, which can be useful, theatrically. To varying degrees, perhaps, but minor characters are as necessary as color tones are to a painter."

The obvious result of this accumulating of everyday incidents, as well as Goldoni's marked dislike of emphasis, is not the heroic superhuman virtue with which the nobility liked to glorify itself but the average virtues as practiced at work and at home by Pantalone, by the merchants and the people of Venice, with their wives and their daughters.

Faults and weaknesses are brought to light solely within the framework of human relations and daily encounters. They are social rather than personal problems.

Goldoni's humor springs from the unavoidable clashes between convention, reactionary attitudes, and social injustice (all "unnatural" attitudes, according to Goldoni) on the one side, and heartfelt truth on the other. A humor that is not satire (in opposition to modern satire) because it is based on tension and conflict. It remains irony and never turns into sarcasm. The classical principle *ridendo corrigere mores* (to correct the situation with laughter) was brought to fulfillment by Goldoni. All faults can be corrected. His comedies have happy endings.

So removed from the workings of polemics and mass indoctrination was Goldoni that even his pacifist antimilitaristic convictions were expressed with wit and humor rather than in a proselytizing mode. This is to be seen in the comedy *The War*. During the curtain call, the actors stress equality of rank, thus symbolically reducing the military virtues of the different nations to the same level of practical futility while wishing "peace to all nations."

In Goldoni's opinion man must prove himself in everyday life, from which there is no escape, be it into heroism, farce, or idyl. In the course of a day, a variety of circumstances forces his characters to lay down their cards. Their words and gestures are totally candid, without preconception or secrecy. One can say fairly that Goldoni never attempted to portray dramatically that part of a person's life that finds expression in the silence of the mind rather than in dialogue.

Completely new to the Italian theater was this method of using typical everyday reality as the source of variety, vivacity, and a freshness that is forever new. These are pictures of life much more than preconceived actions. They contain enough psychology, characterization, color and atmosphere, even a musicality all their own, to draw a valid diagram of real life, and they have enough vitality to set the pictures in motion.

4. Goldoni's Language

Even modern research and the latest stagings, in Italy as well as in other countries, have never paid sufficient attention to the language of Goldoni's theater and to the contribution that Goldoni made to spoken Italian throughout Italy.

"May my audiences prefer simple language to preciosity, and nature to the straining of the imagination," said Goldoni. This attitude pervades all aspects of his work, and cannot be stressed enough. It also underlies his language, which is as far from the *purgatissima lingua* of the academy as it is from the vulgar abstractions of the *arte* actors. At the core of his dedication to language, one sees his recognition that Italian could only be revitalized through attention to the meaning of words. He set himself the goal of banishing from drama the fantastic, the gigantic, the declamatory, and the rhetorical.

Goldoni's language was taken from everyday life, as were the subjects of his plays. The result is a clean and careful popular language, which is extraordinarily effective theatrically and very speakable. Its authentic vitality proves valid to this day when one compares the dialect he used to the dialect still being spoken by the inhabitants of Chióggia (then called Chiozza).

In the beginning, his style was still somewhat formalistic, as, for instance, in *The Servant of Two Masters*. But there is no trace of this in his later works. In his persevering search for the spoken language, he became increasingly aware of class-distinguishing characteristics, milieus, conduct prompted by social class, and the variety of ways by which man expresses himself. No one before him took this approach to language. And no one has been more skillful at portraying the respective social class beyond the individual character so concisely, in a few lines, by means of language alone, while simultaneously integrating voices and responses into a well-orchestrated whole.

This typically Goldonian procedure and its artistic result, can certainly not be classified as naturalism. His selection and stressing of what is typical is genuine, realistic poetry. It is realism in its best and fullest meaning.

The frequent use of dialect in Goldoni's comedies is not surprising. It falls neither into the category of satire (which dialect was used for in pre-Goldonian theater) nor into that of strained local color. Venetian was simply Goldoni's native language, one in which he felt at home and with which he could work the best. It was for him the most vital means of expression.

If one considers the elasticity that Italian dialects have maintained, and the marked distinction between educated and popular Venetian that is still being made in the Venice of today, one understands the significance of Goldoni's Venetian being used as a "language" rather than as a "dialect," in the pejorative sense of the word. It had valid currency in northern Italy, in the *salons* as well as in the streets.

To Goldoni, language had not only the same importance as action but also prompted the action, in the broadest sense. It has been said that Goldoni's main characters are first of all linguistic creations. This statement may be expanded to mean: From the first sentence on, the language of each character establishes his attitudes, his background, and his social class. No character is ever isolated, not even at the moment of his first appearance, and the four walls of his house, solid though they may appear in the set, do not enclose and separate him.

One item of value borrowed from the commedia dell'arte is the rhythmic flow of dialogue. In Goldoni's hands it evolved from the commedia's formal effect, into a kind of lyricism, born of the given situation. His dialogue never loses its function as action-prompters.

The commedia dell'arte was created by mimes for mimes, with the accent on gesture. For stock characters, words are unnecessary. Goldoni, however, always "speaks" his action, which is prompted by the quality and character of his dialogue. If the language is not respected, the play is destroyed.

5. Goldoni's Portrayal of Society

It is characteristic of Goldoni's comedy that it moves on several levels and that it defies limitation by classification. The concept of character comedy must especially be called in question, since Goldoni never used a single main character to carry all of the action.

Goldoni himself once said that, unlike the French, Italians would not settle for a single main character.

His statement agrees with the general Italian notion that man cannot exist outside the context of family and community.

This interrelated communal life (in contrast to Nordic aloneness, the need to isolate oneself for solitary decisions and reflection) corresponds fully to Goldoni's view of the world and explains the chronic structure of his plays. He painted no social outsider in comic or reflective human situations. He did, however, introduce characters lacking those virtues essential for a profitable, reasonable community life.

An example of this focus on the group can be seen in his treatment of the way injustice is responded to. He never offered a fanatical avenger of injustice (in comic version, of course). Instead, in *Much Ado in Chiozza*, he conveyed the distrust of authority traditionally harbored by the fishermen of Chiozza, one that leads them to prefer to settle matters among themselves. (These were not matters he satirized. Goldoni himself denied that he wrote satire.)

In view of his understanding of the *theater* as a luminous reflection of the world with all its mobile many-sidedness, Goldoni's work should be called not character comedy but "a comedy of character."

The world and the theater. Neither of the two is considered or treated as a separate entity. Equal attention is given to both. It is critical observation, translated into effective theater. It is a living stream that carries people's lives and preoccupations back to the people (the audience) in the form of a pleasantly thoughtful work of art, conceived within the framework of a new theater technique that is ingeniously controlled.

It was the only way to free Italian theater—and in particular Italian comedy—from all the obsolete layers entombing it and from sterility. A true *risorgimento* was brought about, a rebirth in its fullest meaning.

Obviously the evolution of the Goldonian theater did not happen all at once. Nor did it by any means follow a straight course. It is an old tendency, born of laziness, to identify a writer with his beginnings, which inevitably leads to schematization and rigidity. Such an approach is in complete opposition to the spirit of Goldoni, whose art always strived for expansion. When he used well-established types and masks at the beginning, he also injected them with life. The plots he devised at the beginning of his career were admittedly conventional but never lacked the vitality of reflecting contemporary society. Only a superficial observer would feel that he detects superficiality and moral as well as artistic stagnation in these early plays.

It is necessary then to interpret even the early plays properly. Later, a social meaning is added to the action, and became more and more evident as the use of masks gradually diminished and finally disappeared altogether.

Skillfully drawn characters took the place of lifeless abstractions, and their effective actions on stage permitted the theatergoer to form conclusions about what was going on in the world. Goldoni was still groping for the world, still striving to analyze it. (For me, the main thing is always the truth, he said.)

In his more mature works, the world itself finally created and permeated the characters and their behavior patterns. The world was no longer discernible as a backdrop. It actively walked on stage in characters who are the images of itself.

Goldoni's stylistic liberation was accompanied by a clear understanding of tangible social situations. In turn this development led to his taking a polemical stand against reactionary attitudes, in life as well as on stage.

Dialogue between stage and audience approached a

hitherto unknown topicality, containing in it a spark of explosiveness. But it never slips into drab proselytizing. This would not have corresponded to events in Venice. Nor would it have been true to Goldoni's own nature, which tended toward friendly pleasantness (comedy, not satire), nor to his concept of art, which had no room in it for the ponderous and the weighty, whether in word or in action.

Ridendo corrigere mores. The span from smile to laugh has many shadings, and Goldoni made full use of it. Anyone he aimed at, either negatively or positively, knew that he had been hit. There was a certain nobleman who thought he recognized himself in the slanderer Don Marzio (*The Coffeehouse*). There was Carlo Gozzi, who assumed the defense of the entire nobility and became Goldoni's most venomous attacker. And there was also the middle class, which saw itself on stage with its faults and its virtues, and the common people, who had never been given their hour on stage before. Nobility, clergy, women, servants, the middle class, and the common people: a fluid array of social categories, offering themselves on stage in the interplay of daily encounters.

The aristocracy does not fare well in Goldoni's work. When he portrayed the protagonists of the dying feudal rulership as useless, he was as accurate as he was outspoken. The degenerate parasitic noblemen, who live off state and church, and the rich braggarts, who have the means to buy themselves a title, are, of course, easier targets than high aristocracy. Still, the many new, always varied contacts that spring from the constant meeting of representatives of different social levels illustrate the decline of the class as a whole.

At the beginning Goldoni used well-aimed polemic intentionally. Later he developed enough detachment and independence to abstain. His noblemen became mere fill-ins that no longer play a significant part in the action. This clearly shows Goldoni's social evaluation of them.

During these years, Goldoni's total confidence went to the middle class, with which he felt connected. He trusted that this class would someday produce other codes and customs, based on reason and on humanity. That it would take over the old aristocratic hegemony and establish a new morality to replace anachronisms and unnatural attitudes.

But there was another social class, the clergy, which Goldoni could not portray on stage. Equally forbidden to him were those who ran the government. Considering that the clergy counted six thousand members in Venice alone, the social importance of this "certain black-robed society that does not practice marriage" (to use Montesquieu's pointed definition) becomes self-evident. More discreet than Montesquieu, Goldoni complained: "Comedy drinks at a large source, but some of its richest tributaries will not let themselves be touched."

6. Women, Servants, the Middle Class, the People

Women are given special importance in Goldoni's theater. Whether servant, mother, or daughter, they are his special beloved symbol of the bonds between private and social life. But they also stand for the polarity that exists between the two, and which Goldoni would have liked to see overcome.

His women are always the guardians and defenders of the "truth of the heart." They are the most natural embodiment of this truth and easily recognized as such by audiences. They are by no means subdued or submissive, not even when Goldoni was dealing with strictly family matters. His respect for the basic rights of any human being clearly shows through all the fun and teasing.

Goldoni was neither a theoretician nor a philosopher. Nor did he take it upon himself to herald a specific social program. His critical observations of human behavior (and of the time in which he lived or of the changing social structure) led him to artistic conclusions in which emotional commitment predominates. This was close to his own nature. And his sparing style makes his characters all the more convincing.

Who then could be better equipped than a woman to express Goldoni's undogmatic conclusions, to voice his unauthoritarian opinions with friendly firmness? It goes without saying that Goldoni's women emphatically insist on their equal rights. Human beings with faults and weaknesses, credible beings of great feminine charm, they could be contemporary depictions of women of our day. They are not intellectuals, they speak from the heart. Goldoni portrayed his women with so much affection that, whenever the action is centered around them, however briefly, all the other characters are caught in the quality that emanates from them, one which communicates itself to the audience.

As for servants, it has been observed that Goldoni, unlike the French writers of his day, treated simple people with great affection.

This is an important statement. Goldoni bestowed human dignity upon the lowly, who had, up to then, been subjected on stage exclusively to ridicule and handled dramatically in ways that demeaned them.

To show *gondolieri* on stage was shocking enough, but it was downright revolutionary when Goldoni endowed the most despised social class, the notoriously starving servants, with flesh and blood. When he made them into thinking human beings whose value judgments undermined the foundations of the existing social order in the name of human equality.

This does not mean that Goldoni's theater lacked clever or simple servants. (Especially not in the beginning.) Such servants appear quite often, but the content of their parts expands more and more, and their eloquence is restrained only at the point at which additional eloquence would be out of keeping with their characterization.

Audacious for his time was his manipulation of the sensibilities that had become a fashion reserved to the higher social classes. To make his point he exemplified these where one would least expect to find them—in the words and deeds of Corallina, in *The Loving Servant Maid*.

The servant team Marton and Picard in *The Well-meaning Grouch*, whose human dignity is as firmly rooted as that of their master, marks the conclusion of Goldoni's evolution toward real humanity.

The middle class was the class to which Goldoni belonged and in which he felt at home. He was at ease with them, and freely dispensed praise and criticism. He did not have to place ridiculous characters outside the confines of Venice in order to ridicule them, as he had often been obliged to do when he drew authentic caricatures of the nobility.

It is a generally known fact that the main part of his work points to the middle class as the necessary active force in the newly forming society. (Its basis is being formed by the merchant class.) He places unlimited confidence in this middle class, whose faults he considers temporary and open to correction.

This is not the place to follow the character of Pantalone through all the phases of Goldonian development, tempting though that might be. Goldoni took the character from masked comedy, in which he had played a funny, even a wicked figure for a long time.

He made him into the representative of the Venetian burgher, the symbol of the middle class (with all its faults and preferences), as well as the exponent of his own views. He fashioned him into a totally new, articulate figure in the history of Italian theater.

It seems more important and more interesting to mention the extensive evolution that the portrayal of the middle class as such underwent in Goldoni's theater. He started off with confrontations between the middle class and the aristocracy, whose uselessness is rendered more obvious by comparison to the able merchant and his healthy common sense.

In the next phase of Goldoni's theater, conflicts within the middle class itself are brought to light and are solved with unreserved optimism by the burghers themselves, thanks to their innate virtues. The faults that bring about these conflicts usually fall into the category of old-fashioned attitudes. Most often these faults derive from customs and behavior patterns that evolve from imitation of the nobility (which remains unmentioned at this point, but the audience recognizes the allusion nonetheless). Or they are various aspects of "generation gaps" and "marital problems," which all go back to the feudalistic notion of the dictatorial head of the family. But there are also stubbornness, avarice, and pettiness—"the occupational vices" of the merchant that tend toward backwardness rather than toward progress.

In this way Goldoni recorded and mirrored the position of the Venetian middle class, a class potentially capable of dismantling the old social structure but one not yet able to tackle the problems that had arisen out of its own evolution or to implement the changes in the social and political conditions that were necessary. Of course Goldoni could not overcome defects of such magnitude within the as yet only evolving middle class. Although he recognized the problems rationally (and that is the final point in his portrayal of the middle class), he could not solve them rationally. That required theoretical reflection, and Goldoni was anything but a theoretician. He merely tried to throw the full weight of his optimism onto the scale, not without a trace of divine melancholy, the *divina malinconia* of his *Summer-vacation Trilogy*, for instance, the melancholy common to all great writers of comedy.

At the end, Goldoni the rationalist opted for the arational power of the emotions. *Love, if you want to be loved!* With this statement he stands on the threshold that leads from the eighteenth to the nineteenth century.

The common people, finally, literally and in many respects, play a part of their own in Goldoni's theater. Up to this time, the man and woman on the street had been but a means of amusement on stage, a subordinate instrument that was never permitted to act independently. (The exception to this is the aforementioned Angelo Boelco, who has been unjustly ignored precisely because of his interest in peasant life and literature. Also, a handful of English dramatists treated the common people with respect.)

Goldoni gave people equal rights on stage. He allowed them to express themselves. In his work they are no longer realizations of tendencies and feelings that had been handed down to them from a superior class. In Goldoni's work the people are never merely objects—not the townspeople in the square or at the windows, not the vendors, not the fishermen. Sympathy and affection for the people are ever present in Goldoni's work.

Goldoni did much more than conduct a loving lyrical examination under the heading of equal rights (humanly as well as theatrically), based on the law of nature. He went further. *Much Ado in Chiozza* is the last great comedy, the last that Goldoni wrote in Venice. (Once separated from his milieu, he could not develop any further in France.) In it, the people have become the firmly anchored subject of the action.

Goldoni left the merchants' middle class. He realized the ideological character of the problems that the Venetian middle class posed for him. Yet, he could not solve them ideologically. A limit was set for him, which he hoped to overcome by expanding his theater to include a totally different social level. Into the more open, more spontaneous world of the common people. In response, the common people enthusiastically recognized themselves on stage. It matters little that Carlo Gozzi's ill-humored aristocratic pride condemned Goldoni's recognition of the autonomous existence of the people in his theater.

Stylistically, *Much Ado in Chiozza* is astonishingly ahead of its time by more than a century. The sparing language and strong characterization point to the verismo of a Giovanni Verga.

The themes of Goldoni's comedies, his stand against the outmoded feudalist behavior of the nobility, his praise of the thoroughly decent, industrious merchant, his subsequent turning away from the middle class that threatened to drown in inner contradictions, his discovery of the rich spontaneity of the common people—all mirrored the dramatist's personal development. His development was a direct reaction to his careful observation and his awareness of social situations. (Without the unjust harshness of black and white, but with a full spectrum of colors.)

It has been said that a sociological study of Goldoni's theater is absolutely indispensable. His concept of life as community life led him toward the social group rather than toward the individual. The long-awaited dialogue between stage and audience had finally been brought about, and the audiences generally accepted it in all its vitality.

7. Rivalries

In the wings of Goldoni's theater, or rather, in opposition to it, stood the conservative static *literati* of Venice's Granelleschi Academy, founded in 1747 and devoted to preserving the purity of style and language of earlier writers. The Granelleschi Academy had no achievements of their own to show, but they sharpened their tongues and their pens against the unorthodox, not particularly well-educated, Goldoni, who dared to bring the spoken language on stage and had the arrogance to reform the entire concept of comedy with the help of a troupe of ex-tightrope walkers.

Carlo Gozzi joined this opposition. He came from a background of impoverished nobility, was a hypochondriac, and became a bitter enemy of Goldoni's theater because it was derived from real life and had social implications that he found particularly repulsive.

Calling Goldoni a *scrittore da fogna* (a sewer author), Gozzi commented:

> He often portrays true nobility as a mirror of wickedness, whereas true rabble is made into living models of virtue and responsibility in a number of his comedies. I suspect (perhaps overmaliciously) that he did this in order to win the favor of the lower classes which are forever rebelling against the necessary yoke of submission. . . .

Gozzi was also hostile to the reform, as his *A Very Strange Story* (*Marfisa bizzarra*), *A Bird of Beautiful Green* (*Augellin bel verde*), and *The Deep-Blue Monster* (*Mostro turchino*) eloquently demonstrate. He even attacked the study of mathematics and the sciences, which he called "one of the vilest plots against humanistic learning and the sanctity of traditional thought lore."

Gozzi's attacks on Goldoni were ideologically motivated (Gozzi's political intrigues were a decisive factor in Goldoni's moving to France), and were directed against the man as much as against the artist. Gozzi did not wish to see reality on stage. He wanted just the opposite, because the general public, namely the people, must not be stimulated or encouraged to think about the present. If we believe Benedetto Croce, Gozzi's plays were the result of an "intellectual bet," by which he meant to prove that "anything" was good enough for mass audiences, even fairy tales.

Gozzi, according to the literary and theater critic Giuseppe Ortolani, "would have preferred not to have been born, yet he had to live eighty-five years to witness the triumph of the very revolution he had fought with the stubbornness of a Don Quixote, all alone against Voltaire and Rousseau, against philosophy and European encyclopedism. He was the irksome Cassandra of eighteenth-century Venice."

This is not meant to be an evaluation of the sometimes ingenious, always bizarre ideas of Gozzi's fairy-tale scenarios, which were always given lavish stage productions. The pertinent point here is that Gozzi was trying to refurbish and repolish the commedia dell'arte. (He left the widest margins for improvisation.) In this sense, his theater may be considered the last caper of so-called improvisational theater.

The Gozzi-Goldoni controversy took place on an artistic level, but Goldoni's other rival, the abbot Chiari, was a downright swindler of the theater, a literary adventurer in the true meaning of the word, whose forgotten, insignificant works do not deserve being thought about today.

The competition with both men—to which Goldoni was compelled by the public's constant demand for new material, as well as by financial insecurity (authors who wrote for the theater were paid little, and only by the work)—understandably, however, led to a few slips, such as his use of Martellian verse and occasional indulging in literary fads. This, he felt, he had to go along with for material reasons. Such compromises can hardly blur his overall image.

8. Goldoni's Dramatic Technique

It is Goldoni's lyricism and his moral point of view that give him a special position in the Italian theater of his time. To him, life and art were inseparably bound together. He saw art not as a matter of contemplative leisureliness or as an escape, but as bound up with life in a very special fashion. Theater, to him, was a form that could teach life as well as entertain.

His plays have not only their special spirit, their very own atmosphere, but also their particular Goldonian lyricism. Goldoni's best comedies make no introductions in the usual sense. His characters are immediately presented, and their main qualities quickly highlighted. In the course of the action we get to know them better and better.

Artistically we might compare this technique to a musical composition, in which the main theme is indicated in the first couple of measures. It is then worked out, amplified, expanded by contrasting voices, further developed toward a climax, and ultimately brought to a finale.

Goldoni's comedy is musical in structure. The director becomes a conductor who indicates the cues, the tempi, the dynamics and tone color. If one searches for an analogy in music to the lyricism of Goldoni, the work of Vivaldi, the Venetian composer, would have to be mentioned first (even before Mozart). His plays have a rhythmically musical order (especially, although differently, *Campiello* and *Much Ado in Chiozza*), the key to which lies in the composed cadence of the text. (And not, as Italians all too smugly affirm, in the innate richness of Italian idioms.) Through the coordination and overlapping of voices and short, well-paced pauses, harmony is achieved.

Another equally important instrument of expression, which is often overlooked in Goldoni's theater, is movement as such, and the direction of movements. His sparing text (and I repeat: his sparing, sober text, all falsified translations and adaptations notwithstanding) consciously left space for gestures and movements, not only as an illustration of the text, but as its congenial complement. Goldoni's theater required that its actors be able to handle body language as well as lyrical language of a high order.

The artistic acrobatics of the Arlecchino in *The Servant of Two Masters* (and in anything in which *arte* characters still appeared, in the early days of Goldoni's theater) is different from the natural (not naturalistic) pantomime of, for instance, the cobbler Crespino in *The Fan*, where it is subordinate to the play. The movement communicates itself to the entire stage. (Differently, yet always present, from *The Servant of Two Masters* to *Much Ado in Chiozza*, the latter being a perfect example of the concept of a stage in motion.) A choreographic arrangement without dance. Movement occurs in one particular spot, becomes general motion, builds, and ebbs away. It is a visual score that the actors must be able to control if the production is to be Goldonian theater.

Goldoni makes full use of every theatrical possibility. His harmony is born of difference, his lyrical unity of manifoldness. Content and style are in perfect accord. The choric concept of the subject matter finds its expression in the choric structure of the play on stage. The individual's absorption in family or community corresponds to the total absence of a star actor. (Goldoni's emphasis on ensemble acting is extremely modern.) The need for a formally disciplined performance corresponds to the subject matter. The ease with which his roles can be acted, which makes the make-believe totally credible (Goldoni surpasses Molière, in this respect), corresponds to his concept of humanity and naturalness. It is his manifold lyricism that makes Goldoni's theater into a perfectly harmonious work of art.

9. The Staging of Goldoni

Goldoni did not know how widely his comedies had spread outside of Italy during his lifetime. He was also spared the exact knowledge as to the manner in which they had been spread. From a purely statistical point of view they were successful. Nicola Mangini, who is director of the International Center for Goldoni Research, reported: "From 1751 to 1800, three hundred and three (printed and unprinted) translations into fourteen languages have been discovered. They are, in order of volume: German, Spanish, Portuguese, French, Greek, English, Dutch, Hungarian, Russian, Danish, Polish, Swedish, Norwegian, and Serbian."

But these sober statistics change into a mirage when one starts looking at the quality rather than the quantity. Goldoni reached the aforementioned language areas mainly via the still surviving troupes of the commedia dell'arte, and therefore "he appeared to the actors as well as to the audiences of the various countries not as the reformer of the Italian theater, still less as an antagonist of the old masked figures, but, on the contrary, as one who was continuing the commedia dell'arte." This, wrote Professor Mangini, explains much of the adaptations and the extremely arbitrary stage versions.

It was as though the remaining *arte* troupes that were swarming through foreign countries had nothing more urgent to do than to take their revenge on Goldonian theater. Since they were totally lacking in new ideas they simply used Goldoni's comedies as scenarios around which they twined their clowning. Outside Italy nobody understood what was being said anyway. Words had never been important to the *arte* comedians, all that counted was the mime effect.

In addition, eighteenth-century Europe identified all of Italian theater predominantly with the commedia dell'arte, and Goldoni's comedy was lumped in with the rest.

His work was not translated, which would have communicated his qualities faithfully. Instead, his plays were adapted, in compliance with the decadent *arte* requirements, and regressed toward trivial farce, always with the goal of box-office success.

This practice began in France while Goldoni was still alive (he knew nothing about it), and was imitated by all the countries Mangini specified. German-language countries later even reexported these falsifications to Italy.

There hardly is another dramatist in the history of the theater who has become open season for producers to such a degree. The liberties taken with Goldonian theater that turned it into a shallow spoof jelled into habit, and some of this habitual attitude has survived to this day. At best, theater convention deemed that Goldoni's plays were mere entertainment that need not be recognized or rendered as art.

It is only since the 1930s that Italian productions began to take a critical historical approach and to respect the original texts, an action that did away with the vulgarizations as well as with the prettifying that had accumulated in the course of two centuries, and restored the original content and form to the plays. An originality that should be met with greater respect and an open mind today.

It is interesting to note that New York critics greeted the Italian-language production of *The Venetian Twins* by the Teatro Stabili di Genova with enthusiasm. Perhaps this is because Americans have little opportunity to see actors specially trained in the commedia dell'arte tradition at work. In any case, the experience is revelatory—*The Village Voice* critic said of this 1968 presentation:

> this is one production which should be attended by actors and directors of all schools. The Theatre of Genoa . . . and their director, Luigi Squarzina, have forgotten more about theatre than most American companies will ever know.

He went on to claim the relevance of the commedia dell'arte techniques to contemporary theater:

> Ad-libbing, sitting down amid the audience, haranguing the front row in machine-gun streams of Italian, breaking into English every now and then, Teatro Stabile manipulates the audience into an involvement which would be the envy of a number of the avant garde's "total theatre" crowd.

10. The Memoirs

In conclusion, a brief mention of Goldoni's memoirs. They are indispensable for an overall picture of Goldoni, even though they have caused considerable misunderstandings when read uncritically. A critical, annotated complete edition has not yet been published.

About Goldoni the man, Mangini wrote:

Carlo Goldoni's personality, his mentality and his morality, has always been presented as an image of kindness, common sense and an emphatically ethical attitude.

The permanent smile on his face expresses a serene acceptance of life and its unavoidable mishaps. The ideal image was projected by Goldoni himself, obviously in keeping with the standards of charm, courtesy, pleasant manners, and serenity that were fashionable during the eighteenth century. It corresponds to the attempt to establish a proper measure of classical harmony and rational morality.

This idealization has led to the well-known misconception that Goldoni was an easy-going man who never felt committed to anything. In the same style of his time (which is alien to us today) Goldoni himself gave a falsified, prettied-up picture of his working methods, as though his intuition had been constant and unfailing, and his comedies had practically written themselves.

It is equally inappropriate to call Goldoni's memoirs his "best comedy," (as it has been called), which is going to the other extreme. His memoirs—titled, *The Memoirs of Mr. Goldoni, for a Better Understanding of the History of His Life and of His Theater*—were written by an aged, tired Goldoni, a Goldoni who had conformed to his day on occasion, who wanted to communicate his intentions and information about his work to posterity with, and in spite of, all fashionable embellishments. His work does, after all, form a unity with his life.

An additional difficulty arises from the fact that he either suppressed certain episodes completely, or else constructed them almost theatrically and fictionally, and that he confused certain dates and relationships. On the other hand, the memoirs also provide reliable indications and corrections. A far more reliable source are his so-called Italian Memoirs, in the Pasquali edition. Unfortunately they do not go beyond the year 1743.

The whole Goldoni in his human, mental, and artistic evolution can, however, be known, understood, and appreciated only after assiduously studying his memoirs and all of his works.

Of Goldoni's vast production an analysis and interpretation of only a few of his comedies can be in this book. Those selected here represent the respective highpoints in the evolution of his theater, beginning with the monument he created for the commedia dell'arte, or rather to the masked character of Arlecchino, going on to his "middle-class comedies," and finally his discovery of the world of the common people.

THE PLAYS

The Servant of Two Masters

Goldoni first wrote this play as a scenario, at the request of the great mime Antonio Sacchi. Only later did he expand it into a firm text, writing out all the dialogue from which the actors were not allowed to deviate.

Goldoni refused to tolerate vulgar expressions and dirty jokes because he feared for the overall concept of his play. He did not want to lose the artistic unity that he had achieved. The story line follows the pattern of simple mix-ups and misunderstandings.

Two lovers (Florindo Aretusi and Beatrice Rasponi) have been separated because Florindo unintentionally killed the brother of Beatrice in the course of a quarrel and had to leave town. Beatrice disguises herself as her killed brother (Federigo), and travels to Venice, where she hopes to find her lover. During the journey she hires Truffaldino (an alias for the masked Arlecchino) as her servant.

Still disguised as Federigo, she goes to the house of the Venetian merchant Pantalone. Pantalone has heard the news of the death of Federigo, who was supposed to marry Pantalone's daughter, Clarice. Because of the death, he arranged the engagement of Clarice to young Silvio, the doctor's son.

Naturally, Pantalone is terribly embarrassed to see the alleged Federigo, all the more since the innkeeper Brighella confirms that the visitor is indeed Federigo. The mystification increases when Florindo, Beatrice's beloved, arrives in Venice and Truffaldino sends him to the same inn (owed by Brighella) in which Beatrice (in the disguise of Federigo) has already taken a room. Truffaldino becomes Florindo's servant as well. This makes him *The Servant of Two Masters*, each of whom is looking for the other without knowing that they are living in the same inn and that they share the same servant.

The twisted situation leads to many comical and tragicomical misunderstandings. At the end, everybody gets his wish: Beatrice gets Florindo, Clarice gets Silvio, and the servant Truffaldino gets the chambermaid Smeraldina.

This is the bare bones of the action, which has no other intention than to create situations. For what purpose? For the timeless spell of theater, for the joy of acting, for people's amusement. In the center stands Truffaldino, who is more than the characterization of an evening's performance, more than a fleeting caricature. He is the embodiment of a being, molded through centuries, the sum total of his Greek-Roman-French-Bergamese-Venetian ancestry, a truly European distillation of naiveté and shrewdness. As stressed by Goldoni, he is a mixture of silliness, derisive deceitfulness, and a passion for gambling. All this as well as being a composite of miserable poverty, timelessness and the genuine essence of all things Italian.

With the exception of the lively chambermaid Smeraldina, all the other characters are less colorful than Truffaldino. Actually, their function is to form only the ring that dances around him. They provide the formalistic *arte* structure that continues the action when Truffaldino does not give it a direct energetic push. This is made clear from the start, when Pantalone (a Venetian merchant with the long thin chin beard) and the *dottore* (usually a lawyer, though he is a doctor of medicine in this play), both of whom wear the indispensable silk mask, contract the engagement of their children in the fixed style of *arte* theater.

In the *arte* theater the style of the language is unchangeable, as is the rapid expressionless delivery, synchronized to the fraction of a second with the complicated traditional gestures. This is the commedia dell'arte at its highest level. A prelude such as this sets the troupe's standard for the audience.

In addition, each masked figure had to comply with the strict register of gestures that tradition had cut out for it. They involved not only the hands and arms but also the legs. During the days of the commedia dell'arte generations of actors were rigorously trained to perform these disciplined movements by their elders. Today, special schools in Italy teach clowning artistry and precision movements. No actor would take on the part of an Arlecchino or a Brighella without having passed at one of these exacting schools.

The modern reader, used to detailed stage directions, may feel the lack of similar directions in *The Servant of Two Masters*. But Goldoni was intentionally staying away from matters that fell within the province of *arte* acting. (A number of Goldoni's early comedies do not indicate whether or not masked figures with their typical gestures are to be used.) In Goldoni's time such indications were superfluous. *Arte* character names and an *arte* vocabulary automatically allowed for improvisation. The *arte* actors had a totally free hand when using scenarios. In comedies with *arte* characters, their freedom was restricted to pantomime incidents, which had the function of underlining Goldoni's text. It was automatically understood that masked characters moved and behaved according to the conventions of mask theater.

On one level, the cast of *arte* characters in *The Servant of Two Masters* functions almost as a background, a colorful background that cannot be genuine unless the acting is perfectly coordinated. It also has the central all-enlivening character of Truffaldino, who acts with and against this background.

Anyone familiar with Goldoni's concept of this particular Arlecchino, as well as with the subsequent evolution of Goldonian theater in an entirely different direction, might suppose that Goldoni had secretly endowed this Truffaldino with the knowledge that he was playing himself in a role that summed up the quintessence of all preceding Arlecchinos, and with the prescience of his impending metamorphosis from a stock type to a real character. Truffaldino plays it with a genuine vitality that precludes all melancholy and only enhances the enjoyment of his action.

Such impressions and thoughts are justified when one looks closely at Truffaldino. He is not a clumsy laughable peasant who is as stupid as he is shrewd. Neither is he a mechanical puppet. He does, on the contrary, know pretty much what he wants. Although his juggling with his double job almost comes to a bad end, he still holds the strings of the action and is superior to his masters. This notwithstanding a symbolical beating. Goldoni characterized him as "uneducated, but extremely bright."

At his first appearance in Pantalone's house he immediately finds out how the persons assembled there are related to one another. While he is talking a blue streak and making his caricaturized obeisances, he observes them closely.

Soon he asks Smeraldina: "Is your ladyship the bride?"

"Oh no, signore," she answers. With a sigh.

Two lines and a sigh masterfully set up the romance between Truffaldino and Smeraldina.

Toward the end of the play, Truffaldino is asked by his master Florindo, who has hardly shown much concern for him, "How will you manage to support a wife?"

He replies: "I'll do my best. I'm counting on Pasquale."

Pasquale is the other servant who does not exist, whom Truffaldino invented as his double to play his own double part.

fantasia

The reply means: "I shall go on serving two masters; I'll earn my daily bread in one way or another." This subtle mockery puts him intellectually several notches above the merely instinctively acting and reacting servant of the commedia dell'arte.

This leads to another concern of Truffaldino, the matter of hunger. It is no longer synonymous with the vulgar voraciousness of the commedia dell'arte. It is genuine hunger, a real matter among servants. It is expressed in this play in a very effective pantomime. Truffaldino tries to reseal a letter addressed to Beatrice (as Federigo), which Florindo unrightfully opened, with chewed pieces of bread. But again and again he inadvertently swallows the pieces.

This bit of stage action also depicts humorously the very real misery of wandering actors. It brings to mind Goldini's description in his memoirs of the way the actors, with whom he had escaped from Rímini, fell upon a plate of macaroni: *"Des macaronis! Tout le monde se jette dessus, on en dévore trois soupières."* (Macaroni! They fell upon it and devoured three tureens.) The omnipresent hunger of the stage servants and the real actors runs through the entire comedy.

Thus we have two main themes interwoven in the

characterization of Truffaldino. One, and by far the more important, is his genuine passionate love of play for the sake of playing. Goldoni endowed him with an *arte* technique and craftsmanship so perfect that it seems to have wings, with *lazzi* (gags) that have not been taken out of the mothballs of an all-too familiar trunk. And they are not arbitrarily thrown in, they are organically fitted into the action. One example is the scene in which Truffaldino packs things by mistake from the suitcase of one master into the suitcase of the other, and vice versa, which must lead to new complications. Or the table scene in which Truffaldino has to serve both masters at the same time and turns into a downright juggler.

The other side is the human being that shows through all the perfectly delivered jokes and through the mask. Yet, this is not a problem play. (Even hunger is not a problem, in the weighty sense of problems as seen north of the Alps, but a way of life.) A human being intelligent enough to play his *arte* game with joy, but at the same time with detachment, who becomes truly great, who becomes the most Italian and the most appealing Arlecchino that ever existed.

Arlecchino, The Servant of Two Masters opened on 24 July 1947 in the Piccolo Teatro in Milano, under the direction of Giorgio Strehler. This first production was followed by two others.

The records of the Piccolo Teatro 1947–1958 contain the following:

> *The Servant of Two Masters* by Carlo Goldoni was first put on by the Piccolo Teatro during the first year of its existence (under the title: *Arlecchino, The Servant of Two Masters*, in order to underline the comedy character for foreign theatergoers) and gradually became a symbol for the

ideological continuation of our work, and for our theater in general.

After a bloody war that brought its inevitable legacy of discouragement and despair to so many people, our *Arlecchino* symbolized eleven years ago the rediscovery of certain eternal poetic values. At the same time the total frankness of the laughter it released, and the pure play of the actors were like a message of hope.

The theater and its actors found again (or tried to find again) the path to the original sources of a theatrical event that had been forgotten in the course of history, and showed to the contemporary public a path toward simplicity, love, and solidarity. The theater rediscovered a glorious episode in its own past, the comedia dell'arte: no longer as an intellectual phenomenon, but as applied to active present-day life. Perhaps it was this particular point that marked the most evident distinction between our own efforts and those of many other interpreters who had preceded us on this path. . . .

Our theater staged three different productions of *Arlecchino*, ranging from the puppet-type stylization of the first to the realism of the third.

The first production was an "intellectualistic" allusion: the actors who were playing the parts of the masked figures, with Marcello Moretti in the lead (that was the time Marcello Moretti began his glorious career as Arlecchino), had the masks painted on their faces.

In the second production, reality took the place of stylization. Marcello Moretti and the other actors with commedia parts wore real masks. . . .

The third production created an Arlecchino who had become completely detached from the intellectualistic concepts of the commedia dell'-arte, which had determined the first and partly also the second production. Now, a group of actors played the story of *Arlecchino, The Ser-*

vant of Two Masters on a stage, with a set that
represented an Italian square in the manner of the
commedia dell'arte.

The set was a completely new creation, based
on a realistic concept, with the dual purpose of
bringing to life again the world of a troupe of
actors and of creating a typically Italian atmosphere.

Arlecchino, The Servant of Two Masters, is,
and is meant to be, the pure audience *diverti-
mento* that Goldoni left as his legacy in memo-
riam to a legendary era of the past, a legacy full
of admirable grace and rhythm, before he em-
barked on the difficult road of reform.

This, then, was the goal of Giorgio Strehler and his
company in their realization of *The Servant of Two
Masters*. They began by reflecting on how to find the
way back to the historically true content and the
genuine art form of the work, which guarantee its
undiminished validity for our time.

As Renato Simoni had done more than ten years
before, Giorgio Strehler followed Goldini's original
text and directions. They worked precisely from a
historical point of view, which led to a new discovery
behind practically every sentence and freed the play
of all the ballast that had accumulated since the end of
the eighteenth century and was responsible for so
much misunderstanding of it.

Goldoni wanted *The Servant of Two Masters* to be
seen as a monument to a national cultural treasure, the
commedia dell'arte in its highest form, and in particular to its most interesting figure, the Arlecchino—or
Truffaldino, as he was called in this play. (Truffaldino
was also the stage name of the famous mime Antonio
Sacchi, for whom Goldoni had created the part.)

For the company of the Piccolo Teatro this meant
first of all an intensive study of the acting methods of

the commedia dell'arte. (In a long, friendly conversation, Marcello Moretti told me that the study turned into a regular course that was not only practical but also theoretical.) Every single type of mask had to be defined; the traditional entry and manner of acting, the typical rhythm of speech and reply, and the movements, had to be studied, as well as the typical gestures, their synchronization with the dialogue, the specific accentuation during the brief moments of silence, and finally, and most important, the masks themselves that some of the actors had to wear.

Ask a contemporary actor of the modern school to wear a rigid mask throughout an entire play that is full of motion! He thinks that his personality will inevitably be lost behind such a primitive instrument of expression. For this reason the actors of the first puppet-type, intellectualistic production had the masks painted on their faces. Attempts made with masks of modern fabrication were technically inadequate. And when Professor Amleto Sartori, the sculptor from Padua, succeeded in rediscovering the method of manufacturing the old Italian leather masks that had been lost for centuries, and the actors of the Piccolo Teatro began using them, it meant that the actor would have to express with his body all the things that would otherwise be expressed with the face; moreover, this with a maximum of control and precision.

But the mouth below the mask remained free and found a different range of expressions. On the other hand it was no longer possible to touch one's mask-shrouded face: such a gesture simply no longer "felt right."

Marcello Moretti discovered a connection between the relatively small openings for the eyes in the old face masks and the peculiar walk of the *arte* figures. Amleto Sartori reported:

Marcello pointed out to me that this type of opening for the eyes reduced the field of vision to a minimum. Therefore movements very rapid in sequence were required. The procedure took place as follows: the actor measures his own radius of action with his eyes; looks down at his feet to keep check on the spot where he is standing to avoid stumbling over a potential obstacle; then he walks in a minimum of space and time.

Such conditions automatically led to an abrupt, jumpy walk, still more accentuated by an almost mechanical movement of limbs and head.

Marcello gave so much rhythm and order to his movements that the figure gradually crystallized and stood out within a firmly outlined architecture, in which each detail was formed and harmonized with the overall concept, which he had grasped with most surprising intuition.

This is how I saw him, and together we pondered. In old engravings and in the entire iconography of the Arlecchino we found Marcello's intuition confirmed. The character always appears fixed in single, separate stages of movement, as on a ballet program, whose sequence Marcello had intuitively recognized.

In order to clarify the historical foundation for the stage existence of the Arlecchino, the living conditions of the Italian comedian must be taken into account. As the critic Luigi Ferrante saw him,

> He knew joy and sorrow, was antirhetorical and antimilitaristic, disturbed the hierarchical order, and took refuge in tomfoolery.
>
> As a repository of misery and especially of melancholy, the Italian comedian bore the traits of his servile living condition and also of a rebellion that reached far into the people: he gave us insights into a violated philosophy that has been

debased almost cruelly to the antilogical level of an agonistic instrument for proving the existence of hunger and injustice the way one used to prove the existence of the soul.

The goal is the discovery of the scenic form by means of the historical development of a way of speech and of popular culture, and that means recreating not only its range of gestures but also its substance, its comical power.

Strehler and Moretti took this approach during their work on *The Servant of Two Masters*, first with the initial stylization (1947), which led to the second production (1952), and finally to the third, in which the set and the directorial concept had been completely changed, now being based "on a realistic concept with the dual purpose of bringing to life again the world of a troupe of actors and of creating a typically Italian atmosphere."

Strehler's direction and Marcello Moretti's interpretation gave no formalistic character to the search for a typically Italian play. Although the Arlecchino tradition, his interpunctuation of word with action, the synchronization of dialogue and pantomime, the isolation of pure gesture to mute expression, was generally preserved, the important point was to restore the historical content and human poetry, to experience them anew rather than to determine their exterior stylization, to kindle them afresh, and rediscover them, filled with vital comedy.

In our opinion, the most important aspect of the three productions of *The Servant of Two Masters* by the Piccolo Teatro is that they can be traced to specific historical periods. To define a character on stage does not mean (as the actors of yesterday, the Goldonians, the great Emilia Zago used to think) to give it life and the heartbeat of the performing actor. Only a critical interpretation is able to reveal the character of a masked figure that has remained the most surprising in the memory of the centuries.

We have good reason today to speak of the general influence critical research has had on Goldonian comedy, of a coincidence of the subjects in the discussion of poetics, and consequently also of the stage realization of a specific text and a specific figure: if one speaks of respecting the written word, for instance, this means that the director and the actors have learned the philological and semantic lesson, not merely that they have respected the comedy in its integrity and have made no cuts.

This is, in my opinion, how *The Servant of Two Masters* came into being, the greatest Goldoni success of recent years, linked to the names of Marcello Moretti and the Piccolo Teatro.

Marcello Moretti had a natural predisposition to accentuate the realistic motives of his acting, which he skillfully pushed to the borderline of the grotesque with totally conscious simplemindedness and an air of buffoonery. The distance permitted the public to participate on the level of intelligence rather than on the level of deception and gave Moretti the feeling "why not call it comic catharsis?" as it used to be understood in the old days.

Until his sudden death in 1961, Marcello Moretti must have played the part a good seven hundred times in Italy and abroad. He was, without a doubt, the greatest Arlecchino since Antonio Sacchi. During the performances at the Piccolo Teatro, one of the rare fortunate coincidences had happened: perfect craftsmanship, artistic skill, and intelligence of the leading actor and of the director had come together in an absolutely ideal blend.

The particular characteristic of the production can once again be summed up as a respecting of Goldoni's text and of the spirit of the comedy. It was *arte* acting of the most technically skilled kind, a group accomplishment harmonized with the utmost precision. In addition, it was a joy of playacting that never failed to convey the impression of spontaneity.

The knowledge of the dual social-historical background (of the *arte* comedians before Goldoni's reform, and of the human being that already showed through the mask of the servant) gave the actors the distance that preserved them from the slightest touch of a formalistic exercise, and gave to their acting the true lyricism that is particularly characteristic of Goldoni and of his modern interpreter Giorgio Strehler.

Of all Goldoni's plays, *The Servant of Two Masters* has been the most frequently produced in both America and England. It is a perennial favorite with college and repertory companies because of the unusual possibilities it offers to modern-day directors and actors. As the program notes for the 1968 Asolo State Theater (Florida) production point out, the play demands "reliance upon the improvisatory freedom and exhilaration of its performers. It is really a kind of contemporary ideal, being both complete and satisfying in form and, at the same time, wildly permissive in content."

The most recent production was that offered by the Equity Theater in 1972, which used a translation by Edward J. Dent. Praising both director and actors, Howard Thompson of the *New York Times* hailed this presentation: "This is Goldoni. And it's gold." In his review he praised the set designer's depiction of "an attractive Old Venice" as being "exactly right," as "the cast themselves flick[ed] trolley curtains providing a tavern, a patio and a courtyard." Admitting that "the plot may seem tatty now," Mr. Thompson described Goldoni as the "playwright whose vivid, literate comedies nailed the aging hide of the commedia dell'arte to the wall forever."

Although English-language productions of the play have frequently been enthusiastically received by drama critics, Goldoni himself has not always fared so well. A 1937 presentation by the Cleveland Play House was summed up by William F. McDermott in the *Plain Dealer:* "The staging on the whole, is better than the material with which it deals." The play itself he described as "a lacy eighteenth century valentine, chiefly interesting as a museum piece. . . . trivial and naive by current standards but not without gustiness, pictorial attractiveness, and the charm of the antique." He criticized Goldoni sharply: "There is no chacterization in this play, no attempt at realism, no imagination."

Presenting plays in modern dress or in costumes of other periods offers directors wider opportunities for interpretation. *The Servant of Two Masters* has not escaped this trend. In recent years, Paul Weidner directed the Hartford Stage Company in a blue-jeaned and T-shirted version. In 1968 Tony Robertson directed an English production at Queen's Theatre in London using Regency (early-nineteenth century) costume. The *Sunday Telegraph* critic discussed this phenomenon in his review:

> changes of period must be justified. Modern dress is always permissible; all other deviations only if they provide some special illumination in the case of an over-familiar work. I suspect that it was the conjugal manipulations and the dominant concern with money that suggested that Jane Austen period to Mr. Robertson.

Nevertheless, the critic concluded that the costuming was "at odds with the spirit of the play."

Beatrice, the heroine masquerading as her brother in order to facilitate the search for her lover, Florindo, is a breeches part. Striped stove pipes— not to mention a moustache—go ill with her exalted sentiments. If these are mocked, the balance of the play is fatally disrupted.

The Servant of Two Masters has not escaped adaptation by contemporary playwrights. One may conclude from reviews that these productions have been exciting, if not always true to Goldoni. A 1971 presentation by the John Drew Repertory Company in East Hampton, New York, was based on "a free adaptation with music" by Barbara Damashek and Kenneth Cavander. This version used lines from *Romeo and Juliet* in the romantic scenes. The *New York Times* critic, though expressing reservations about the nature of the adaptation, commented that "while frequently deserting Goldoni in dialogue, the show is faithful to him in spirit. . . ."

A 1971 Canadian production by Halifax's Neptune Theatre was based on a new adaptation by David Turner, who gave the lines a cockney flavor. The *Ottawa Citizen* termed the presentation "rollicking" and "hilarious," and praised the updated script: "once you get used to it, Mr. Turner's way with the dialogue makes for a lively evening and sweeps away any cobwebs that may have been hanging around 18th century Venice."

In 1960 the Piccolo Teatro troupe toured America with the Giorgio Strehler production of *The Servant of Two Masters*. Even though the play was presented in the original Italian, New York critics were unanimously enthusiastic. The expertise of the acting and the quality of the staging attracted their acclaim. Walter Kerr of the *Herald Tribune* praised the incidental improvisational acting:

One of the most charming things about the Piccolo Teatro di Milano is the way the actors behave offstage. We are, as it happens, given a chance to see both offstage and on: a gay central trestle takes up only the heart of the acting area, with all sorts of room for idling performers beyond.

The *New York Times* critic called the Piccolo troupe "a consummately trained unit" and attributed the fact that the language did not act as a barrier to "the antic quality of the piece and . . . the shameless abandon of its slapstick." Marcello Moretti's acting of Arlecchino was invariably singled out for special praise.

Richard Watts, Jr. of the *New York Post*, while appreciative of the Piccolo Teatro rendition, had some doubts about the nature of the play itself:

I suspect that you might have trouble keeping up with the plot maneuvers of Goldoni's classic 18th-century comedy. And, even if you managed it, I doubt if its ancient conventions of story and character would seem especially amusing any longer. With the Piccolo Teatro's presentation of Goldoni, the manner is everything and the narrative is very little.

"A strange phenomenon, a fluid cross between the most abstract geometry and creatural exuberance"—this is one of the multitudinous ways of defining the commedia dell'arte, that unique theater that bloomed in Italy from the sixteenth to the eighteenth century. At the core of this theater of improvisation and masked stock characters was the much-loved Arlecchino, the quick-witted servant who masterminded his masters. Starting out as a playwright as the *arte* theater was coming to its end, Goldoni used the ingredients of the Arlecchino character to create a comic masterpiece—*The Servant of Two Masters.* *Above*: Ferruccio Soleri portrays Arlecchino in a 1963 Piccolo Teatro production at the park of Villa Litta, near Milan. Directed by Giorgio Strehler.

PICCOLO TEATRO DI MILANO

Going to Venice to search for her beloved, Beatrice (played by Polly Holliday), disguised as her dead brother, hires the incomparable Truffaldino (left; played by Donald C. Hoepner) as her servant. (Truffaldino is the name Goldoni gave his Arlecchino character in this play.) Pantalone (center, played by David O. Petersen), the Venetian merchant, is another stock character from the commedia dell'arte. Photograph of production of *The Servant of Two Masters* by the Asolo State Theater in 1968.

WAYNE MANLEY

Opposite, Brighella, the lovable rogue (left, as played by Charles Carusi)—another stock character from the commedia dell'arte—and Truffaldino (right, as played by Steve Itkin) are probably hatching out a plan of putting something over on Truffaldino's two masters. The quick-wittedness of the peasant characters was a staple of *arte* theater. Photograph of production by Tufts Arena Theater in 1970.

DUETTE PHOTOGRAPHERS, ARLINGTON, MASSACHUSETTS

The Mistress of the Inn, surely one of the most delightful comedies ever written, has unfailingly charmed audiences for two hundred years. Mirandolina, one of the most fetching heroines who ever stepped across the boards, is a merry-hearted wench who sets herself the challenge of conquering the embittered misogynist Cavaliere di Ripafratta. All this while running an inn and holding off two noblemen who feel a fatherless girl of the common people is fair game. The Cavaliere surrenders, but to no avail. The game is over, and Mirandolina will marry Fabrizio, a man of her own class, as her father wished. *Above*: In this famous ironing scene, the love-smitten Cavaliere stands by, while Fabrizio estimates what it will take to master the spirited mistress of the inn.

JAY DEE
TEXAS CHRISTIAN UNIVERSITY, SCHOOL OF FINE ARTS

Below: Mirandolina (as played by Laura Cox) stands amid her four suitors—the Conte d'Albafiorita (as played by Robert Sessions), Fabrizio (as played by Charles Ballinger), Cavaliere de Ripafratta (as played by Charles Jeffries), and the Marchese di Forlipopoli (as played by Jamie Greanleaf). Scenes from a production by Texas Christian University Fine Arts Festival in April 1961.

Of his *Summer-vacation Trilogy*, Goldoni wrote that the first play, *Summer-vacation Mania*, focused on "the frenzied preparations"; the second, *Summer-vacation Adventures*, on the "antic life-style"; the third, *The Return from Summer Vacation*, on the "dire consequences." The sober ending to what starts as a wildly funny comedy contains Goldoni's warning to the Venetian middle class of what abandonment of real values leads to. *Opposite:* A scene from the Piccolo Teatro di Milano production in 1954, directed by Giorgio Strehler.

STUDIO FOTOGRAFICO DEL PICCOLO TEATRO DI MILANO

Much Ado in Chiozza dramatizes the fracas that arises over a slice of baked pumpkin. So heated becomes the controversy in this tiny fishing village that the matter is brought to the magistrate. But as the day ends, the community settles down and turns its attention to the planning of three weddings. In the scene *below*, the magistrate, Isodoro (as played by Mario Valdemarin), hears Toffolo, the town simpleton (as played by Corrado Pani), tell his side of the story of the afternoon's heated battle. Produced by the Piccolo Teatro di Milano in 1965 and directed by George Strehler.

LUIGI CIMINAGHI, STUDIO FOTOGRAFICO DEL PICCOLO TEATRO DI MILANO

The protagonist of the aptly titled play, *The Fan*, is indeed a fan. Before it reaches the hand of the one it was intended for, it has evoked all the passions of man as it travels by misunderstanding and mischance from one character to another on every level of society. Here the disconsolate innkeeper Coronato (as played by Michael P. Keenan) laments his experience with the fan to the vain, impoverished Conte di Roccamonte (as played by David O. Petersen). Photograph of production by the Asolo State Theater in 1967.

THE ASOLO STATE THEATER, SARASOTA, FLORIDA

The Fan

Pure misunderstanding from the start, with perfect unity of time and place. The protagonist is an object that causes so much turbulence that one might think it were alive: a cheap fan.

This play was written rather late, after Goldoni had gone to France, after his evolution as an artist had long since reached its high point. At that time he was working on a level that had hardly anything in common with *The Fan*. But one must keep in mind that Goldoni suffered an artistic setback when he went to the *comédie italienne* in Paris. There he was expected to write only improvisational theater for the Paris *arte* ensemble.

This atmosphere, coupled with his lifelong theater experience, produced a play that must be ranked with Goldoni's early works solely because of its structure. But as to originality and artistic perfection, it stands in a class all by itself (which has not been equalled since).

People occasionally claim that vaudeville, skits, and such are closely related to *The Fan*, since they imitate the mechanics of this joyful comedy. In this play, however, the action is never absurd. Neither are the characters puppets that move to the sounds of a carillon—they are living creatures of flesh and blood.

The set is the recently built neighborhood of a village: the workshop of a cobbler (Crespino), the general store of a woman who has recently moved in from the city (Susanna), a pharmacy (with Timoteo), an inn (with Coronato), a small café (with Limoncion), a farmhouse (with Giannina and Moracchio), and a small villa, the summer house of Mistress Geltruda and her niece Candida.

Candida's fan falls over the parapet of the terrace and breaks. Evaristo, a young man from the city who is in love with Candida, buys a new fan from the shopkeeper Susanna, and asks the peasant girl Giannina, who works for Candida as a maid, to give it to her mistress.

This starts a regular odyssey of the fan, which practically passes through everyone's hand: from the cobbler to the innkeeper, to the count, to the baron. It is snatched, stolen, given away, sold. It causes confusion, hatred, envy, jealousy, pains of love. It pits the nobility against the middle class, the common people against the middle class and the nobility, and finally reaches the tender hand of the one it was intended for.

But shortly before it does, as though to prove it has an existence all its own, it spins the thread of the comedy and of the story one more time, this time in a word dance that goes from mouth to mouth:

> EVARISTO (to Susanna): Signora Susanna, do you recognize this fan?
> SUSANNA: Certainly, Sir. You bought it from me this morning. And I, fool that I was, thought you had bought it for Giannina. . . .

EVARISTO (to Giannina): Why did I give you the fan?

GIANNINA: To give it to the Signora Candida. But when I wanted to give it to her, she started scolding me and wouldn't let me talk. I tried to give it back to you, but you didn't want to take it, so I gave it to Crespino. . . .

CRESPINO: And I fell, and Coronato took it.

EVARISTO: Where is Coronato? How did he lose it?

CRESPINO: Hush. Don't call him. Since he's not here, I can tell the truth. I was angry, so I went to the inn to get myself some wine, and I happened to find it there, and so I took it.

EVARISTO: And then what did you do with it?

CRESPINO: I gave it to the Conte, as a present.

BARONE DEL CEDRO (disdainfully to the Conte): You got it back then. . . .

CONTE DI ROCCAMONTE: Yes. And I returned it to Signor Evaristo.

EVARISTO: And I presented it to Signora Candida.

This gives a brief outline of the confusion, of one side of the comedy. Characters and movement make up the other equally important side.

Twice—at the beginning of the first act, and again at the beginning of the third act—the scene opens with pure pantomime. Both are indispensable for the style of the play. (Here Goldoni gives explicit stage directions.) They are beautifully composed, and form points of rest before and within the many brief sparkling scenes of this comedy, one that Goldoni said was to be performed with constant action and continuous movement.

But that is not all. They introduce the characters to us during the first silent scene as they act in usual ways: we see the innkeeper pluck a chicken, the peasant girl as she sits spinning outside her house, the ladies from the city sitting on their terrace.

A summer day in a village. A variety of subjects has been worked into this watercolor with light brush strokes. In pairs, in a variety of groupings, they move about on the stage as the day takes its course. The evening brings rest and fulfillment after the day's turmoil.

It is the summer-vacation subject on a middle-class level. Aunt and niece are spending a proper fashionable summer vacation in the country. Evaristo goes hunting, which is an equally fashionable activity. The moving about of the lively fan directs the romance of the young people.

But the type of response they experience is not only completely different from the reaction of the nobility or of the common people, but is also different from Goldoni's earlier portrayals of middle-class lovers. This facet alone tells us when *The Fan* was written. Goldoni no longer depicted the middle class with forcefully optimistic brush strokes. The measured Geltruda, who has only the interest of her niece at heart, may still correspond to the positive notions with which Goldoni had earlier endowed his middle class, but Candida represents a new, more pallid generation. Candida and Evaristo are presented not with the colorlessness of the ever present lovers, usually a dull enough pair in the tradition of the commedia dell'arte, but with the pallor of approaching romanticism.

In the evening garden (certainly with a moon and a sound of crickets), unnoticed by all, the lovers' reconciliation begins when Candida faints and Evaristo sinks to his knees. (Goldoni was so discreet that he only offered a report of the scene.)

Evaristo is depicted more clearly. His sole occupation is to be elegant (a far cry from the formerly depicted productive middle class) and in love. He is somewhat naive, nervous, and easily excited. He, too, might faint in a given situation. He is, in embryo, the fatal heartbreaker of the coming century.

The new neighborhood of the village symbolizes the present. Far beyond somewhere stands the feudal estate, whose anachronistic representative, the ruined Conte di Roccamonte, who demonstrates his vain usefulness all through the play, still considers the members of the lower classes his serfs. The comedy has no main character, but the Conte hovers through the entire action. "We title bearers," is his favorite expression, and his title is his sole source of income.

His resemblance to Don Marzio (*The Coffeehouse*), and more so to the Marchese Dry-bones (*Mirandolina*) is unmistakable. A scrounger of shallow grandeur, who reads with a flourish yet excels in ignorance, who has the cobbler repair his no longer reparable shoes, who finagles invitations to dinner and coffee, who receives a few free barrels of wine, two pistols, and a golden snuffbox in exchange for poor matchmaking, who always joins the winning party in the end, upon which he bestows his illusory "protection."

Goldoni set the play near Milan because of the wretched Conte, but he, as well as all the other characters, are clearly Venetian. The common people move through the everyday life of this comedy in a way that is totally different from the noblemen and people of the middle class. They are rendered forcefully, unmistakably. They are sure of themselves. In spite of all their teasing, horseplay, and jealousies, they distinguish themselves from the others, as Goldoni intended that they should as the healthy positive element.

The good-humored cobbler Crespino, who wants to make a better life for himself with the work of his hands; the self-assured innkeeper Coronato, who gambles his livelihood; the young peasant who stubbornly and quite unsuccessfully tries to arrange a marriage between the innkeeper and his sister, who is in love with the cobbler. And finally the girl Giannina herself, one of Goldoni's most successful women characters. She is irrepressibly vivacious (a splendid contrast to Candida), insouciant and friendly, always ready to throw her distaff at the head of any unwelcome caller in a sudden fit of temper; as primitive as she is impish, and thoroughly appealing.

To this village beauty all people are equal. This irreverent girl, with a natural nobility of soul, is a match even for the affected mannerisms of the Conte, whom she tells off in a delicious, unforgettable, and well-deserved fashion.

In between stands Susanna, the shopkeeper from the city, an inquisitive gossip who thrives on intrigues, who finds village life too monotonous. A foreign body in the village, who typifies all the "followers" of the fashionable summer-vacation trend.

Limoncino, the clever coffeehouse waiter, who has much in common with his colleague in *The Coffeehouse*, is still tied to *arte* acting. His part is only subordinate and complementary.

Barone del Cedro, another fill-in, has no direct influence upon the action. He serves merely as an aristocratic conversation partner in dialogues with the Conte, who puts him down. The Conte pushes him into the foreground as a potential husband for Candida. He hasn't a chance from the start, though it looks as if he does, of competing with the middle-class Evaristo.

This brilliant comedy shows a cross-section of all levels of society. The visible confusion caused by the will-o-the-wisp fan notwithstanding, it has a carefully thought-out and precisely composed inner and outer structure.

The mimes of the *comédie italienne* did not understand the parallel harmony of content and form. (Goldoni sent the play to Venice, where it was performed with great success.) Caught in the sterility of routine acting, they did not even see the genuine theatricality of *The Fan*. An insignificant object that changes hands and prompts a chain reaction of misunderstandings, which are more or less funny, but all credible (this was Goldoni's claim). One such incident is the caricatured but not vulgar chase at the end of the second act, which is intentionally reminiscent of the commedia dell'arte. Even the pharmacist (Timoteo) trips and falls with all the perfumes he had prepared for Candida.

What lyricism is hidden in these images that move past us in rhythmic motion! Motives and characters are only hinted at, the substance is only touched upon —this increases the charm and makes for natural lightness and flow. From a pantomime that is acted by everybody on the entire stage, to dialogue skillfully characterizing every single person, from the conversation in the street that leads to a window, and from the window back to the street; and finally to the big chase.

It is the harmonious coordination of all of these theatrical elements that make in their totality the perfect work of art.

Of this play a Goldoni scholar wrote:

> The choice and brief sketching of the motivations, and their coordination into the visible disorder of reality and the real order of art, reveals great craftsmanship. Perhaps this is the only one of Goldoni's comedies in which the light and mobile description of the milieu and the sharp yet brief sketching of the human character are so perfectly blended.

The Fan opened on 15 July 1936 at the Campo Zaccaria in Venice in a production directed by Renato Simoni and offered during the XXth Biennale.*

Renato Simoni has the great merit of having been the first to bring Goldonian theater back in its original form. At this point all artificiality had already been dropped and replaced by the world of the eighteenth century as it really was, not as it had been posthumously fabricated.

Of this performance the drama critic of *Il Corriere della Sera* wrote:

> Life pulsates here from the very beginning, full, warm, strong, funny, amusing to the highest degree.
>
> Renato Simoni's ingenious direction has succeeded in revealing the characters and the full charm of Goldonian comedy in their authentic essence. Simoni has proved himself to be an intelligent and patient restorer of *The Fan*. He carefully removed the dust and mildew that had gathered on the master's image over the years, and more than that, he also removed the additions of former bad restorers, the nonsensical corrections, the strangest distortions, the ingrained improvisations with their apings, their stilted caricatures.
>
> Once again the picture shines clear and beautiful in its original colors, with its accents, perspectives, its chiaroscuro, and its humorously dropped repartee in the nimble, quick, and totally vivacious mobility of comedy.

* The Venice Biennale, primarily a festival of the visual arts, incorporated theatrical performances into its activities between 1934 and 1941. In 1948, a special division of the Biennale, the International Theater Festival, was instituted and was called the IXth festival to stress its continuity with the earlier eight years of theater performances organized by the Biennale.

In this production, which Luigi Pirandello went to Venice to see, the famous eighty-year-old Ermete Zacconi played the part of the Conte di Roccamonte.

Of his acting the *Il Corriere della Sera* critic wrote:

> The sober, controlled comedy of his acting turned into an unforgettable artistic creation. All of the mannerism of the vain salesman of illusion is contained in his *Oui, Madame*, produced in the inimitable tone of the great actor during the second act, after he asks Signora Geltruda for the hand of her niece Candida in the name of the Barone del Cedro, and Signora Geltruda asks in return: "Is the Signor Barone in love with my niece?"
>
> And in the third act, when he cons Evaristo out of a snuffbox worth fifty sequins, to make the baron return the fan that he himself had given to him, Zacconi's splendid performance was greeted by storms of applause.
>
> Each individual actor deserves great praise for his performance, but the unity and balance of the entire company is above praise.

The critic F. Palmieri raised a number of interesting points:

> How should Goldoni be performed? There exists a tradition of performing Goldoni against which we have frequently protested, because it always confused style with mannerism, friendliness with affectation, the emphasized soberness of dialogue and characters with the sweet sounds and curtsies of alleged eighteenth-century artificiality. . . .
>
> Renato Simoni's direction strictly adheres to the text of *The Fan*, a proof that our Venetian author needs no helpers, no more or less disinterested ideas. His freshness is rooted in the spirit of his characters, in the humorous lively dialogue.

Simoni's successful direction is what he wanted it to be: smooth, clean, and spoken. Goldoni must be truthful, as he intended to be. There is no need to imprison his dialogue in languid speech cadences. . . .

Italian theater was born in the eighteenth century, of the un-mannered, dry, colloquial plastic Goldonian prose, without beauty spots and without academicism.

In order to offer faithful Goldonian theater, Renato Simoni, critic, playwright, and director, not only followed the original text (adhering even to Goldoni's stage directions, including the silent scenes) but also took the cue for his direction mainly from the word itself. Strehler used the same method. And like Strehler, Simoni was not satisfied with his first production either. Three years later he followed it up with a second, also in Venice, and with a new cast.

Anything that had been too abstractly formalistic in the first production (Strehler called his first attempt with *The Servant of Two Masters* too intellectualized), as for instance the pantomime episodes, became still more true to life, while the necessary rhythm and the differently balanced characters of the various scenes were strictly maintained. Simoni's carefully weighed, sure direction was able to reveal the typical even in incidental occurrences (even a slight unsureness in the precision of the sketching can destroy the image Goldoni intended). Now it was mainly geared toward simplicity and truthfulness.

The Fan has not been so widely produced in the United States as *The Servant of Two Masters* or *Mirandolina*. College drama groups and repertory companies have accounted for most of the play's American exposure.

That the possibilities are promising for English-language presentations of the play was shown by the 1966 British production at the Pitlochry Festival Theatre. Hailing the performance as "brilliant" and "ravishing fun," *The Stage* critic praised director Jordan Lawrence, who successfully maintained the play's impetus and timing to evoke "the volatile, gay Italian spirit. At the very best moments, it is hard to believe one is not hearing the play in its original language. . . ."

Singling out stage designer Daphne Dare for special mention, the critic described the two-tiered stage settings that provided a flexible background to the action:

> The teeming bustle of shopkeepers and tradesmen at work in front of their little shops, the social interplay between petty grandee, bourgeois and peasant classes, is compressed and yet uncompressed, so that the vivacious story unfolds with the grace of a flower and the flash of a fan.

Mirandolina: The Mistress of the Inn

Mirandolina: The Mistress of the Inn is Goldoni's best-known comedy, but probably also the most abused. Some producers have turned it into a farce. Others have endowed it with the conventional mannerisms of a labored rococo style, embellishing it with an abundance of frills and fans, powder and lorgnons, that make it into a kind of splashy bit of entertainment. To add insult to injury, this particular style has been known as "Goldonian" since the last century. (More recently even a man like Georges Pitoëff totally misunderstood the comedy, and staged it with much clowning and with somersaults. And Jules Lemaître has called it "simple-minded.")

To begin with, *Mirandolina* is a portrayal of feminine psychology, dramatizing the quintessence of the art of seduction.

About it, the writer and theater historian Silvio D'Amico wrote:

Think of the countless Don Juans that have come to the stage since Tirso.* They all show the adven-

* Tirso de Molina was the first to introduce the Don Juan legend into formal literature. His gripping drama, *El burlador de Sevilla*, was published in 1630.

tures rather than the seducer's art. We are never shown how and why Don Juan casts a spell over women. It is never explained in detail. His charm is assumed and accepted from the start. Whereas *Mirandolina* demonstrates exactly how the seducer tackles the stubbornness of the woman hater, how she bends it, shakes it up, breaks, and finally conquers it. . . .

That in itself is a very special accomplishment.

As in all great Goldonian comedies, all of which are more interested in the how than in the what, the story line is the simplest in the world: Mirandolina, the owner of an inn, obeys the last wish of her dead father and marries her servant Fabrizio.

But before she does, she has to fight off the Marchese di Forlipopoli, who, though destitute, assures her of his so-called protection, and the Conte d'Albafiorita, who showers her with expensive gifts. There is a third aristocratic hotel guest, the hitherto embittered woman hater Cavaliere di Ripafratta, and he is the one whom Mirandolina forces to his knees.

Like all great Goldonian comedies, this one has no prelude either. From the first scene on, situation and atmosphere are clearly set up. As the play continues, more details come to light. From the start Goldoni lets us into the rivalry between the Marchese di Forlipopoli and the Conte d'Albafiorita, which runs through the entire action like a continuous thread.

There is another important point that is overlooked in most stage productions, and that is the social climate. This is also made clear from the very first scene, and it was especially noticeable to contemporary audiences. In spite of its psychological validity, the lady innkeeper's seduction game, with its subsequent misunderstandings, would lose its solid ground without the social overtones.

Here is the situation.

A young single woman owns a hotel that, although unpretentious, is altogether acceptable to higher-class guests. The word gets around. Two noblemen come to court her, not because they want to marry her, God forbid (that would be improper, and unthinkable, a social abyss lies between them), but because they are on the lookout for adventure, for a relationship without consequences, for an easy prey. Thanks to their social status, they think they can get it.

Again, the characterization of the two noblemen is so piercing that Goldoni had to place the action in the vicinity of Florence. Two typical representatives of the idle Venetian aristocracy. It was written when the Republic had just issued a public though futile appeal, asking the members of the aristocracy to try working once again, especially at commerce, to which Venice owed her greatness.

Goldoni hit the nail on the head when he ridiculed the old decadent, desiccated nobility, which no longer exercised any function whatsoever, and the new nobility, whose younger generation was squandering the fortunes their fathers had painstakingly accumulated. (They are the equivalent of today's playboys.) The basic antagonism between the two groups is understandable.

There is a good reason for the play to open with the words: "There is after all a difference between you and me." This is what the young Conte d'Albafiorita is told by the Marchese di Forlipopoli, a representative of the old aristocracy. The comedy soon finds a nickname for the marchese, which has remained proverbial in Italy to this day: the Marchese Arsura (literally: dried up; the Marchese Dry-bones).

He owns scarcely more than his title, and he peddles it and thinks that it will win him the favors of Mirandolina, as well as of any other woman who crosses his path. It does gain him a free lunch, offered by his rival. In addition he is an avaricious coward. A perfect caricature of the bankrupt, stuck-up noblemen that ran around Venice in droves.

The Conte d'Albafiorita, with his purchased title, is another matter entirely. He relies on the power of his money, giving Mirandolina many presents, especially in public, to shame his rival into making similar presents. This reduces the Marchese to utter destitution. Whereupon the Conte lends him all of thirteen sequins, knowing full well that he will never get them back.

The Conte's character is no better than that of his rival. When he notices that the Cavaliere di Ripafratta seems to be successful with the lady of the house, he tries to soothe his injured pride by bribing the other guests to move elsewhere at his expense.

The Marchese and the Conte pay persistent court to Mirandolina, without being in love with her, of course. They serve as the juxtaposition to the main theme, to the game the lady is playing with the third nobleman, the woman hater.

The unfortunate Cavaliere di Ripafratta is a better brand of human being, and not only outwardly. (His title is as exclusive as it is solid; he goes back to the old order of knights.) Unlike the other two he is not caricature material; he is the central serious comedy figure. He is unwittingly comical. He hates women, but without going to extremes. He distrusts them on principle. He is particularly afraid of being tied down. This automatically forces him into a defensive position. Otherwise he is rather pleasant, and soon explains his basic philosophy to the Marchese: "Respect others if you wish to be respected yourself!"

But when his infatuation over Mirandolina is exposed, he is seized by a wild rage. He must deny his capitulation. He smashes a water pitcher at the feet of the Marchese and of the Conte. "I'm ashamed to listen to you a moment longer without telling you that you're a liar!" he screams at the Conte.

This is the traditional formula that triggers the duel with which noblemen settle their disputes. The Cavaliere is, after all, in the worst possible position. Only flight can save him, at the end of the comedy. Mirandolina has humiliated him. He is more than ever convinced that women are false.

The Cavaliere is basically a decent man. Unlike the other two, he has no impure motives. He is not looking for an adventure with Mirandolina. (His brief conversation with the two actresses shows that he is not unfamiliar with their kind, that he may even have had a few fleeting love affairs.) But he could never have married Mirandolina, not without jeopardizing his title. He simply lost his head, completely, with open eyes, unable to defend himself against Mirandolina's artful seduction. The awakening at the end is bitter, almost tragicomical.

Various stagings and adaptations have omitted the two actresses as superfluous. Goldoni sketched them only rapidly, and they do not stand out as characters. But they are necessary. The light sketch of an actor's life charmingly loosens the action just at the right moment. It only *seems* to lead away from the action. Of course, we can consider the actresses who arrive at the inn under false aristocratic names independently; they become a humorous episode of alienation. The dramatist smiled about the "art of survival" of actresses of his day, and then forced them to play caricatures of themselves.

They are poor girls, basically, whose beauty makes for a better attendance when they sit evenings in the box office. And they are willing to clean suits on the side for a scudo a job. "They are just traveling folk. Thus friendships need not last and the men don't lose their shirts. . . ."

But Ortensia and Dejanira have a precise function within the play. They further add to the characterization of the three noblemen, each of whom behaves differently toward them. More important, they represent a much weaker mirror image of Mirandolina's acting talent, which stands out all the more sharply. What dilettantes these professional actresses are by comparison!

Mirandolina's game lasts only one whole day, the last day of her unrestricted freedom. Born of an ambitious caprice, it becomes a crucial test at the end. Cleverly, it is a test for the audience more than for the actress who plays Mirandolina, if we may, as an exception, make the following reservation. From the start, Mirandolina has both feet on the ground. She knows exactly what she wants and what she does not want. She manages her inn with skill and circumspection. In an emergency she is a better cook than her cooks. She knows how to win the respect of her servants, supervises everything, does her own ironing to make sure that her laundry is impeccable, keeps her own books. In a word, she is a capable young lady who displays in her profession all the good qualities that Goldoni expected also of middle-class men.

In the history of the theater Goldoni mastered a long road in a short time. From the stereotyped chambermaid, via various Columbines, Corallinas, and Smeraldinas, to this independent Mirandolina. Her comfortable sense of her own social worth is revealed by her skillful way of holding her own, as a commoner against the aristocracy.

We must not forget that people who did not belong to the nobility were still called "the people" in Goldoni's time, when the middle class was only just emerging. Mirandolina is characterized as a person representative of this newly emerging class, as is Fabrizio, the highest staff employee at this inn, who will enter a higher social level when he marries Mirandolina.

Mirandolina's pleasantness toward her guests is part of her competence. We easily understand that she accepts presents from them "because she does not want to hurt their feelings." But she keeps aloof. When these "caricatures" (as she calls them) want to pay her court, she feels flattered. But even the Conte has to admit that he has not been allowed to touch as much as a finger, in spite of all his expensive presents.

That is the striking part about this Goldonian creature; with all her joy of life and her delight in teasing she always behaves decorously. Mirandolina has been having a bit of fun, without impairing her dignity. And she does triumph, even in her risky game with the Cavaliere. The defeat to which she confesses is sheer pretense.

Lady-killers like the Marchese and the Conte are ordinary everyday characters to her, men who confirm her charms. A wave of her hand, and they come running. She can just as easily send them away if they become too persistent. (Toward the end they become so persistent that they want to secure for themselves a lien on Mirandolina's marriage, with wedding presents of protection and money. She asks them politely to look for another inn.)

The Cavaliere, on the other hand, is a genuine challenge. A woman hater? "The poor fool. . . . What man can resist a woman if he gives her enough time to deploy her charms? Sooner or later he has to surrender, whether he wants to or not."

She knows how to handle him. "You're quite right. Don't change your mind. Women, signore. . . ." She only confirms his mistrust of women. She is never sentimental. Instead, she bases her entire game on frankness, just enough frankness to be taken for honesty, but not enough to be genuinely honest.

A little extra attention: the finest bed linen, a personally prepared dish, a few deprecatory remarks about the other two—"What do you think of the weakness of these two noble gentlemen?"—a shared glass of wine. At the end a few tears and a feigned fainting spell, and the fortress falls.

After that there is nothing but mockery and humiliation. The little golden flask, which she refuses at first and then crossly accepts. The splendid ironing scene, in which she tells the Cavaliere in Fabrizio's presence, "I do like him, you know. . . ." And at the end, when matters have almost come to a duel (because the Cavaliere will not admit to the others that he has fallen in love), there is her confession: "Yes, I tried to turn his head . . . I carried on and on. . . ." What deeper humiliation for an inveterate woman hater?

These are only the main elements (scheme, triumph, and humiliation), each of which corresponds to each of the three acts. It is impossible to render the feminine psychology with which she proceeds, the way every word, every gesture fits. She is supreme in her art of seduction. A false step, tactically as well as morally, would be ruinous. It is precisely the combination of youth and playfulness and absolute integrity that makes her so appealing.

Mirandolina's relationship to Fabrizio is on another plane. Dramatically, it represents the counterplay to her main design on the Cavaliere. On this plane she sees, on the one hand, the end of a phase in her life. On the other she calculates with feminine practicality: "Such a marriage promises after all the security of my interests and position without curtailing my freedom." No one before Goldoni dared tell such a truth—not even in a monologue when a woman might be honest with herself.

It is clear that Mirandolina is marrying for practical reasons. She will maintain her social position, and Fabrizio knows the inn business. It is equally clear that she hopes to dominate the marriage. This is how her determination to keep her freedom is to be understood, not in a lascivious sense, which would be totally out of character.

Mirandolina plays with Fabrizio partly to delay the marriage on which she has already decided (before she marries, she wants to accomplish her masterpiece of conquest), and partly to prepare the future climate of this marriage. She gives him clearly to understand that she is the mistress and he still her servant. And at the end, when he is about to flare up she flatters him diplomatically, thus binding him still more strongly to her.

Under the circumstances, Fabrizio cannot be an insignificant character. It would make the denouement that Goldoni intended mechanical and destroy the play. Fabrizio is not a deus ex machina, an *arte* character that appears at a given moment because the play needs an ending. The part of Fabrizio is more than instrumental, it is completely independent. But it is subdued so that the main theme of this single day emerges in sharp brilliance.

The only real servant in the play is the Cavaliere's valet. This is an expansive part, in spite of its brevity, and because of the contrast it supplies it should not be omitted.

Fabrizio is more than just a servant. One takes him seriously from the start. In contrast to the Marchese and the Conte, he is by no means a caricature. To judge by his behavior he might almost be taken for the owner of the inn. It is natural that he evaluates the guests according to their tips. (Mirandolina also accepts presents.) He shows a considerable amount of dignity and firmness. Reprimanding the Cavaliere, he says, "What is all this noise! This is no way to behave in a decent inn."

Again to the Cavaliere: "Your excellency is paying for honorable, legitimate service. But you cannot expect a respectable woman to . . . You asked her to come to your room. . . ."

An ordinary servant could not afford to take such a stand against a nobleman without being beaten on the spot. But Fabrizio is only ordered out of the room. One does not beat Fabrizio.

He is also sure of himself as far as Mirandolina is concerned. We cannot be so sure that she will always wield the power. The famous ironing scene is intended for him as well as for the Cavaliere, and with all the emotional ups and downs he does not (in contrast to the Cavaliere) come off second best.

The words he says to himself—"She has a mind of her own, but I'm fond of her"—are far from simpleminded. They are full of understanding and self-assurance. And at the end of the play he proves that he is quite capable of imposing his will at the decisive moment, calmly and firmly. Before committing himself to marriage, he tells Mirandolina: "I'd first like us to come to an understanding. . . ."

Mirandolina understands. She turns to her aristocratic suitors and says: "Please be good enough to look for lodgings elsewhere. . . ."

This comedy is another example of the concertlike structure of Goldoni's theater. The accent is on the different tonalities, the voices and qualities of the different characters, while the group action is maintained.

The various characters are lightly drawn. As the action continues, they are gradually expanded and paraphrased, but in such indissoluble harmony that critical analysis should remain incomplete. Attention to individual characterization strikes one as an act of sabotage against Goldoni's intention. And if one voice or another is omitted in a stage production, or in some way separated and isolated from the vital naturalness of the overlapping and fusing, things must in the end go to pieces.

The different tones of the dialogue, which is the focus of everything in this play, are more important than ever. Nothing is allowed to detract from the dialogue. The number of characters has intentionally been limited to a minimum. Set and costumes are secondary auxiliaries, accompaniment rather than foreground elements. The dialogue leads the characters to the action. They themselves seem to create the situations that contain as much of the unexpected as the theater demands as well as enough verisimilitude to seem true to life.

Mirandolina: The Mistress of the Inn opened in Venice on 2 October 1952 for the XIIIth International Theater Festival of the Biennale. It was acted by the Roman Repertory Company (Compagnia Stabile di Roma) and directed by Luchino Visconti.

Two hundred years after the original premiere almost to the day, Luchino Visconti created a *Mirandolina* in a style so new that it had to have a revolutionary effect. Nevertheless, he did not in any way deviate from the now more and more prevailing historically oriented manner of producing Goldonian theater that is in strict adherence to the intention and the poetry of the unfalsified original.

Visconti's concept is social realism (and not naturalistically neutralized). This is his basis. "The principal key to every state of mind, to every psychology, and every conflict, is for me in this case predominantly a social one, even though the results at which I consequently arrive are purely human, and concern only the individual persons."

It was obvious from the start that Visconti was not going to offer mannered theater of the old school. But such a radically modern performance, such a rigorous dusting off of a masterpiece, came totally unexpectedly. (The critics made comparisons to Louis Jouvet's direction of Molière's comedies, *The School for Wives* and *The Mischievous Machinations of Scapin.*)

While Renato Simoni had pointed out the way with the specific intention of revealing Goldoni's world in all its authenticity and freshness, Visconti's attention was directed mainly to Goldoni's characterizations, to which he gave a modern expression. He made no cuts whatsoever. According to the drama reviewer and director Luciani Lucignani, Visconti was careful not only "to stress certain specific typical cadences and movements in the Goldonian manner of expression but also to endow the characters with an honesty and a truthfulness that astounded us at times so much that we had to look at the text to convince ourselves of their authenticity."

In other words, Visconti's direction proceeded from the social background of the characters and the social basis of the play. Its middle-class realism is therefore taken for granted. Perhaps he also refrained from emphasizing it because Goldoni's outlining demarcation of the four social groups represented here is not sufficiently worked out. The attention is thus focused on Goldoni's theatrical structure: development of the action, situation, and atmosphere on the basis of the dialogue, paraphrasing and harmonizing of voices and movements with the expression of natural spontaneity, integration of all theatrical elements into a poetic unity.

Visconti rendered all of this with full authenticity, although with such extreme modernity as can still be defended. He did away with every trace of bric-a-brac, not only in the set but also in the pantomime, which might lead the actors as well as the audience toward unwanted directions. For instance, the attributes of a fashion (beauty spots, reaching for the snuffbox), which seem hardly natural to us today. Thus, the gestures, and the word before them in its creative function, and all compositions and dissolving of moments, reach a clarity that strikes us almost as ascetic. This approach is derived from Goldoni's special talent, which portrayed and intensified persons and characters from the outside. (He used no music. Once a church bell strikes a few times in the distance.)

But Visconti's essential contribution lay in the way he blended the effects of light, costumes, and set, an additional poetic element subordinate to the action in the Goldonian sense.

It is known that Goldoni's contemporary, the painter Pietro Longhi, was closest to Goldoni's art. And if Goldoni's characterizations occasionally reveal a line that leads via Verga all the way to us today, Pietro Longhi permitted visions that lead via Goya to Morandi.

Visconti and Piero Tosi, who collaborated on the sets and costumes, used this interesting affinity between Longhi and Morandi for their sets and costumes. Their successful experiment was, in spite of the calm it radiated, an artistically exciting symbiosis.

Theater and film critic Giulio Cesare Castello wrote about this production:

> Morandi's style dominated the performance with its calm clarity, with his neutral soft shades, predominantly beige, Havana brown, and off-white; with his geometric, clear, orderly, extremely simple lines.
>
> The three scene changes—the little terrace of the inn high above the rooftops of Florence, the bare, yet immensely warm room, the airy laundry room filled with blue sky and pieces of wash hung

up to dry—are sheer miracles of selectivity, functionality, and chastity of expression.

As soon as the curtain rises on any one of these so essentially modern scenes, which are completely without extras or embellishments, one realizes that the *Mirandolina* that is being performed here is not the traditional one but another.

To avoid misunderstandings: Another does not mean that Visconti has faked or overemphasized any essential point. It merely means that he has looked for a different frame, and that, within this frame, he has made his characters move and speak in another manner.

Of the most famous actors, we will mention only the lead, Rina Morelli. According to the literary critic Giovanni Battista Angioletti, Visconti made Mirandolina into

> a creature without gravity, all harmony from the color of her dress to her smile, always completely controlled. He took away the bubbling over, the extreme vivaciousness the part allegedly required.
>
> Rina Morelli may be the only actress who could adapt to this unusual style. Her performance was so intelligent and friendly that it created a hitherto unknown Mirandolina, one who corresponded to the portrait drawn by Goldoni, but was less localized, with more sensitive and poetic gradations, than were the traditional performances.

According to Liugi Ferrante, Visconti's production raised fundamental considerations.

> the new lesson that was being taught the Italian theater was the formal structure of modern art: the functional quality of the stage sets, Morandi's

color tones, simplifications of the costumes derived from Longhi, constantly intellectually controlled acting.

Strictness of form is an elaborately discussed subject of modern art, with which theater reviewers are perhaps less familiar but which is all the more alive among painters and all persons concerned with the graphic arts and with music.

As far as formal attempts on stage are concerned, Visconti went furthest afield, and the endings of his acts, his choric compositions, the concert of action and lighting dynamics, are new acquisitions of our performing arts.

Mirandolina: Mistress of the Inn has been relatively popular in America. The famous Eleonora Duse played Mirandolina on a United States tour. During the 1930s, Eva Le Gallienne's Civic Repertory Company presented the play both in New York City and on the strawhat trail. In a 1937 production at the Westchester Playhouse, New York, Miss Le Gallienne directed the play and acted in the lead role. Critic Douglas Gilbert of the *New York World Telegram* found the play still of relevance to contemporary audiences:

> It is an amusing satire, in style quaint now and fan-like, but the essence of its characterizations are still of a piece with the quirks of human nature, for there was a keen observation behind Goldoni's bitter pen.

But Mr. Gilbert was only partly satisfied with Miss Le Gallienne's intepretation of the Goldoni classic; he thought that the production should have been more traditionally styled:

> A broad prank, Goldoni's "Mistress" should be done with ostentatious intimacy. Sometimes this

was achieved in the Le Gallienne production, but seemingly only because of the limitations of the narrow stage, and the confidential asides to the audience might have been more marked, for when the pretension is exaggerated, the preposterous quality of these resuscitations is enhanced and the charm of their comedy increased.

Like other Goldoni plays, *Mirandolina* has lent itself to musical adaptation. But the 1957 musical comedy *The Mistress of the Inn* by Don Walker and Ira Wallach, starring Beatrice Arthur and Jack Cassidy, had little success, and Goldoni himself did not escape sharp criticism. According to *Variety*, the play "should have been left in 18th century Italy. [It] must have been dated even when it was written."

Gentlemen of the Old School

This comedy, little known outside of Italy, was written in Venetian dialect, and the title, *I rusteghi*, is not easy to translate. It has been called *The Ruffians*, a translation that either ignored or else misunderstood Goldoni's own foreword to the play.

In Venetian dialect the word *rustego* was the label for a man who is not only unsociable and unpolished, but also, and especially, behind the times. A man who keeps his eyes closed to the changing conditions around him and clings to customs and ideas that the present considers "barbaric." (Barbaric in the Latin sense, without the implication of "ruffian.") Beyond conveying this characteristic of uncouthness because of conservatism the rather extensive complexity of the Venetian *rustego* cannot be rendered.

Goldoni showed the character and life-style of a *rustego* from four different angles, which are all derived from the same basic make-up, and among which family tyranny predominated at the time the comedy was written. One specific character, divided into four, or rather multiplied by four, to quote Goldoni's friend Gasparo Gozzi (a sensitive translator and author, founder of Italian journalism, and the brother of Goldoni's militant antagonist, Carlo Gozzi).

One hesitates at the prospect of synopsizing this play because the main line of action, in the sense of conventional theater, provides only the foundation of the comedy on which everything else has been dramatically constructed.

A brief outline may therefore suffice:

The merchant Lunardo has decided to marry his daughter Lucietta to Filipetto, the son of his friend Maurizio. The two young people are not supposed to know about the agreement between the two businessmen, and on no account are they to get to know each other before the date fixed for the marriage vows.

The first to oppose this old-fashioned attitude is Felice, the wife of one of the quartet of friends, an alliance of domestic tyrants who form a united front of the past and deny all rights even to their own wives. With brilliant wit Felice not only manages to help the young couple but also wins her battle against the guardianship of women and gets the quartet to accept a more modern concept of family and social life.

This simple straight line of action is only the foundation, the point of departure, and not even a very important point at that. The real problem is much vaster. Illustrated by all kinds of allusions, the play portrays the whole crisis in the life-style of the Venetian society of Goldoni's time and its effects upon the families of the middle class. This was the class from which Goldoni had expected a new code of ethics, founded on rational humanity.

Especially after the peace treaty of Aix-la-Chapelle, which ended the War of Austrian Succession in 1748, Venice continued to be receptive to European thought and literature. She gradually began adapting more modern moral concepts, which the women in particular helped implement in daily life. They began going out of their houses more than before, and participated in public events. (They even began to "converse" with artists and writers.)

Fashions were changing rapidly and stimulated increased interest in dress. The patriarchal position of the head of the family was weakening noticeably. Parents began to discuss potential marriages with their sons and daughters of marriageable age, and the engaged couple was permitted to meet, which had not been allowed before. Morality based on feudalistic concepts was beginning to dissolve.

This process was, incidentally, initiated by the progressive members of the nobility who continued to set the trend. Actually, however, modernization was an imported product that corresponded to a general need but for which a social basis did not as yet exist. The Venetian middle class was not able to take even the first step toward a new code of ethics.

Goldoni was obviously committed to the emancipation of women and of youth. It seems doubtful that he still had unreserved confidence in the middle class because he kept at a distance from his characters, in spite of his familiarity with their background. (From an artistic point of view this is only an advantage.)

With a subtle smile Goldoni depicted the reactionary quartet. A kind of compassionate detachment led him to try to improve morals by exposing them to smiles from his earlier effort to improve morals by eliciting laughter. Analysis and synthesis succeed all the better for it. The world and the theater fuse into a unity in which the social contrasts and weaknesses are also the contrasts and weaknesses of generations beyond the specific subject.

As soon as the stage silence is broken by the words "Dear mother" . . . "Yes, my daughter? . . ." at the beginning of the comedy, we are immediately in the typical atmosphere of a prosperous middle-class home, complete to the traditional knitting and the chronic stinginess, and as a contrast, the only remotely sketched carnival time. A restricted environment.

Lunardo, the master of the house, has not yet come home. Nevertheless, he controls the scene, which is his creation. The four walls, the locked doors, and the shutters imprison him no less than his wife (his second; Margarita) and his daughter (by his first wife; Lucietta). They are talking, while dutifully knitting and spinning. They do not even know what there will be for supper, because the master of the house insists on doing the marketing himself.

This delightful scene between young stepmother and the stepdaughter, who is in her late teens, immediately sets up the reactions of the two to the reactionary concepts of the husband and father and also establishes the relationship between the two women. The atmosphere and the theme of the play can be felt from the start.

About this play the writer and critic Manlio Dazzi wrote:

> [*Gentlemen of the Old School* is] too inexhaustible for any kind of comments. [It is] a living organism in which all moral, social, lyrical, and theatrical subjects, characters, mentalities, and behavior fuse into such essential unity that the analysis of any separate part must seem like a vivisection.
>
> All the things that take place in the dialogue, the constant juxtaposition of temperaments, themes, actions, moral crises, family upbringing, relationships between parents and children, and between marriage partners, between the old and the new, between past events and new ambitions,

could set off an exegesis that would, by its extent, destroy the vital spontaneity of genius inherent in this work.

The play is the ideal realization of the *comédie sérieuse* in the Goldonian sense. It is a comedy that wants to be taken seriously, that lacks any allusion to the traditional *lazzo* (or jest). It no longer follows the methods of conventional theater that always placed a negative character in juxtaposition to a positive character.

In other words, Goldoni avoided the opposition of black and white, and endowed all his characters with varying degrees of negative and positive qualities. Even the four tyrants have their good points. The resulting comical situations are true to life. In certain spots Goldoni might have been tempted to slip into a *comédie larmoyante* (tear-jerker), but he by-passed this danger with a detached smile.

The fact that Goldoni approached his characters and subject matter as always from the outside, drawing them as they looked to others, proved once again to be an advantage. ("Our greatest depth is our skin," Paul Valéry affirmed almost two centuries later.) It permits him many nuances and shadings that illuminate and confirm the basic unity from constantly different angles.

Lunardo is the strongest, most clearly defined of the four domestic tyrants. But he is not any more hateful than the others, in spite of his power mania and his ridiculous secretiveness, his fear of being found out; in spite of the stinginess that makes him prefer heaps of linens in his cupboard to a new dress for his wife. Goldoni disapproved of his conduct and ridiculed him, but at the same time he had as much understanding for him as he did for the others.

The men are not, under the cloak of rationality, exclusively composed of harshness and egotism. Life itself fashioned their hard shell, and a kind of self-discipline that is as much part of another era as is their authoritarian behavior.

Lunardo's speech pattern was formed in everyday business life ("Let's get down to the facts") and is contrasted to the dialogue of his somewhat simple-minded wife, Margarita ("Imagine that!"). Lunardo is trapped in his own hardened shell (a circumstance that is a little sad, in spite of the funny situations). He may conduct his daughter's marriage in a reactionary attitude, merely as a business deal. Nonetheless he loves her sincerely, although in his own fashion.

Maurizio is a greedy introvert; stiff as a rod. To him, happiness consists of saving as much money as possible for a rainy day. But such a rainy day would be a catastrophe for him. Yet he is so fond of his son Filipetto (who is to marry Lucietta) that he takes his side against Lunardo, and defends the very affections for which he bitterly reproaches his son.

Simon is the hardest of the four, the most plagued by avarice and mistrust. He does not wish to conquer the world. He withdraws from it into a fortress. A word uttered without suspicion would be like a slowly lowered drawbridge. It would mean unconditional friendship, and that, to him, would correspond to surrender.

Canciano belongs to a higher social level, he is a "citizen," which is, according to Venetian social ranking, one step below the aristocratic patrician. He is a weakling, even though his ostentatious boredom and his dry gruffness try to give an impression of a kind of black humor.

The quartet must form a united front against the present. They are an irrational power that is doomed to wane from the start. Youth condemns them. Their wives oppose them. They end up realizing that they cannot exist without their women. Their opponent, Felice, uses this "weakness" to advantage. She separates them from each other, isolates them and defeats them with such brilliant logic that they must finally admire her and give her credit.

The women in this play have been disposed in such a manner that the strongest and most intelligent (Felice, who can afford to have as her admirer the Conte Riccardo, an insignificant nobleman who provides the only surprise effect) belongs to the weakest of the men (Canciano), while the least significant (Margarita) is the wife of the firmest of the men (Lunardo).

Lucietta, the bride-to-be, combines naiveté with shrewdness, forwardness with reserve, and displays, moreover, the still slightly angular freshness that is typical only of a girl in her late teens.

Filipetto, the groom-to-be, is not as awkward and childish as he may appear at first glance. He knows very well what he wants and how to bypass paternal authority. Both young people wish only to escape the tyranny at home. And both want the new. The world is getting younger.

Here, too, the dialogue is masterful. With an impression of unreserved spontaneity it presents each of the three character groups (the men, the women, and the young) as having a unity of its own. The unity leads them into the action that creates the moods and the situations. Yet each character has his or her particular manner of speaking that reveals him or her to the innermost depth. Turns of phrases and words indicate the section of town from which each of the "masters of the family" has come (audiences knew what conclusions to draw from such indications). Certain obsolete expressions further underline the situation.

Most critics have agreed the *Gentlemen of the Old School* is a work of perfection so far as composition,

lyricism, and artistic unity are involved. The critic
Natalino Sapegno wrote that this play is "an ideal mixture of subtleness and irony," a "detached contempla-
tion of the passions, faults, and human caprices in the
light of a serene yet genial wisdom."

Summer-vacation Trilogy

These three connected plays—*Summer-vacation Mania, Summer-vacation Adventures, The Return from Summer Vacation*—occupy a special position in Goldoni's work. They were written toward the end of Goldoni's residence in Venice, but before *Much Ado in Chiozza*.

Goldoni had repeatedly handled the summer-vacation subject. He had even devoted five comedies, one *dramma giocoso* (humorous drama), and one intermezzo to it. Among them is a comedy entitled *Summer Vacation*.

As we know, Goldoni liked to write various preliminary versions of a subject or character that was preoccupying him. He liked to grope his way as he went along. The end result is always a masterpiece, the premise of which differs from the preliminary writing and astounds by its novelty. From the point of view of form it would certainly be interesting to make a study of the techniques, environment, and subordinate subjects that were the main subject in the preliminary plays. *Mirandolina* was such an end result, and so was the *Summer-vacation Trilogy*, although on a larger scale.

Within the elastic realm of Goldonian comedy, the *Summer-vacation Trilogy* stands on the borderline between comedy and drama. It concluded Goldoni's rationalist middle-class period with a readily recognizable study of romantic psychology. The triology is a sad, disappointed swan song to the middle class that had not been able to give itself a new code of ethics. All of this is contained in the three morality comedies, which must be understood as an entity.

The subject matter practically offered itself. In the past, the noble families of Venice used to spend the summer in the country (in the beautiful Venetian villas, some of them built by Palladio, the sixteenth-century Italian architect who worked in the classical tradition), partly to relax but also to spend some time thinking about intellectual matters and to occupy themselves with the arts. Now, people were going to the country to amuse themselves, play, converse, flirt, etc. They continued to do what they were doing in the city, but with fewer inhibitions, in keeping with a purely hedonistic life style.

The middle class adopted the aristocratic pattern. The middle-class version is the theme of Goldoni's fresco. The first part shows "the frenzied preparations, the second the antic life-style, and the third the dire consequences," as Goldoni wrote of this trilogy. His social criticism gradually increased in seriousness from the comedy of the *Mania* to the *Adventures*, and culminates in *The Return*.

Two neighboring families are preparing for their departure to the country. They are, on one side, Leonardo and his sister Vittoria, and on the other old Filippo and his daughter Giacinta. Leonardo's critical financial situation does not prevent him from buying a great many things on credit from merchants and tailors. He and his sister want to keep up with the others and show themselves off in style.

At his daughter's instigation Filippo invites Guglielmo, a friend of the house, to go to the country with them. Leonardo, who is in love with Giacinta, becomes insanely jealous. A mutual old friend, Fulgenzio, who transmits Leonardo's marriage proposal to Giacinta, suggests that Guglielmo be disinvited, to prevent gossip. But Giacinta is stubborn, and although by now happily engaged to Leonardo, she insists that Guglielmo come along so they will have a bigger crowd in the country.

In the country all indulge in the fashionable goings-on: cardplaying, good meals, conversation until late into the night, with flirtations and jealousies on the side. Meanwhile, other people have joined the group: love-starved Aunt Sabina (who tries to capture the playboy Ferdinando) and young Rosina (whom the others match up with Tognino, the village doctor's insignificant young son).

In the midst of this modish, basically boring life Giacinta and Guglielmo realize that they love each other. But under no circumstance does Giacinta wish to give in to this feeling. She is engaged to marry Leonardo, and her good reputation would be jeopardized if she were to try to change matters. With quick determination she asks Leonardo in Guglielmo's name for the hand of his sister Vittoria.

Back in the city, all threads converge in a conclusion that is far from optimistic. Hounded by creditors, Leonardo faces total financial ruin. Good old Fulgenzio accompanies him to his rich Uncle Bernardino, who has nothing but biting sarcasm for his squanderer of a nephew, and no intention whatsoever of lending him a helping hand.

The ending simply brings matters to a close. Leonardo and Giacinta move to a remote country estate, which Giacinta's father owns in the vicinity of Genova, and which Leonardo will manage for a living.

But Giacinta has married a man she does not love, and Guglielmo does not love his wife, Vittoria. The doctor's son had to marry Rosina in secret. The love-starved Aunt Sabina promises a considerable legacy to the playboy Ferdinando, who is solely interested in her money, before he agrees to marry her.

Summer-vacation Trilogy is Goldoni's only work that does not offer a solution at the end. Goldoni sees no solution that would be in keeping with the reality of the events, and he is too honest to fake a happy ending, of which the middle class is, in his opinion, no longer capable. In this respect (and especially with respect to the country setting) the frequently made analogies between Goldoni and the theater of Chekhov are certainly of interest. The full dimension of Goldoni's artistic and social scope has never been properly investigated to this day.

The first part of the trilogy is nonetheless still the typical familiar Goldonian comedy, with all the turbulence and all the haste of last-minute preparations, which yield sufficient comedy material. It plays on feminine rivalries about the inexhaustible subject of fashion. Goldoni was in his familiar element, handling subjects he knew well with competence and wit. (The first of the three plays is doubtlessly the best constructed dramatically.) At the very beginning he introduced the principal characters with their essential qualities, and defined their interrelationships. But they all move on one and the same level. Contrasts of mentality are not played out. Juxtapositions of social or family groups, which Goldoni usually pits against one another, are not developed.

In the first play (which could, if necessary, exist as an independent play, because of its form) he introduced an essentially, exclusively middle-class problem, demonstrated by the different characters. Leonardo is a harmless good-for-nothing, completely superficial, and therefore completely without malice. He loves Giacinta from the start, in his own way sincerely. He is jealous and tries to keep up with her in fashion and appearances. He is perfectly aware of his precarious financial situation, but he is a spendthrift and readily relies on the dowry Giacinta will bring him.

In the beginning he is the one who creates the most hectic travel whirl, while in the country he comes into the foreground only when he manifests his not-so-unfounded jealousy. He is never able to talk things over with his fiancée. When his financial collapse is beginning to loom, he leaves on the pretext that his rich Uncle Bernardino is dying and wants him to assume the succession. (He proves this with a forged letter.)

Leonardo is a weakling to whom Goldoni did not give much depth. Back home in the city he does not know how to escape his creditors and the threatening legal consequences. He has to turn for aid to old Fulgenzio. But in the end he has to renounce Giacinta's dowry and to take the only resort open to him—that of managing a rural property of his father-in-law.

Vittoria, Leonardo's sister, is cold and selfish. She is of course aware of her brother's financial distress but does not care about it in the least. The essence of her life is dressing according to the latest fashion and having fun. Living, to her, means to have unlimited time for all the superficialities, which she can, in turn, use to show herself off. Particularly pronounced—almost a vital necessity—is her jealousy in all realms of feminine vanity. Her conversations with Giacinta (who is, after all, her friend) are downright lessons in falsehood on both sides and amply illustrate her character. She wants to marry Guglielmo, and in the end she gets her will.

Goldoni has characterized her only as an example of the general superficiality, of a lack of genuine values, of a relationship to people and to things that is almost unrelatedness. Vittoria is the most selfish character in the play.

Filippo is old and so disarmingly naive that one cannot possibly hold anything against him. He is relatively wealthy, and sees his duty as a father solely in the fulfillment of his daughter's every wish. He belongs to the old generation of merchants who used to go to the country for business reasons and take care of their vineyards. But now he lets himself drift on the crest of the "new," with its modern comforts. He wonders with a funny yet moving helplessness why no one seems to take him seriously even though he is the head of the household.

In the end, Leonardo's threatening bankruptcy does not trouble Filippo much, because Giacinta's dowry has already been squandered, and he is glad to pay off his son-in-law with the administration of an estate he had almost forgotten. He is an old man who has been passed over by the times.

Giacinta is the central figure of all three plays. First of all, she is the object of Leonardo's and Guglielmo's love, and of Vittoria's jealousy. Mainly she is the only one among Goldoni's many women characters whose development provides the significant psychological break that foreshadows the conflict material of romanticism. This young lady who takes pride in making others do whatever her bidding, whose thinking is in no way less selfish than that of the others, and who is, moreover, aggressive and calculating, is suddenly forced to experience the reality of an emotion. Previously, she only pretended to have feelings, and suddenly she is forced to feel the power of love.

This is the actual conflict of the play, Giacinta's inner conflict, rooted though it be in the conventions of her time. Without going so far as to establish a relationship between the character of this young girl, who is the only one of her kind in Goldoni's creation, and Madame Bovary, the second part of the trilogy (and partly also the third), with its country setting, is a turning toward romanticism. Of course the director must be careful not to overemphasize the dramatic impact of the relationship at the expense of the fresco method used here by Goldoni.

Eventually Giacinta confesses her love for Guglielmo, to herself as well as to him. But after her confession she wants to stop the matter (in keeping with her character, which is preoccupied solely with external considerations), to forestall the possibility of gossip. Her engagement is not an unbreakable bond, but she gives up Guglielmo for the sake of her reputation and marries Leonardo, to whom she is indifferent.

Guglielmo, as a counterpart to Leonardo, appears more staid and calm at first. Then, in the country, it reverses. Guglielmo, who is now courting Giacinta, stands in the foreground. He is usually extremely conscious of correct conduct, but now he begins to push the limits of the rules of their society. Thus there is some justification for Giacinta's manipulating him into becoming engaged to Vittoria.

He is not a character in the essential sense either. He is neither better nor worse than the others whom Goldoni has gathered together as the banal representatives of the increasingly shallow middle class. The other middle-class participants in the game serve as amusing variants to the main theme (like the love-crazy Aunt Sabina), especially at moments when the situation might otherwise easily slip into pathos.

Furthermore, attention must be drawn to the servants, who, in contrast to their bored "masters," really enjoy the summer in the country because they have less work to do. As a group they offer a natural, restful contrast to the general boredom. This applies especially to the lovers Paolino and Brigida, who are no more than sketched.

It is further characteristic of Goldoni that, of the two characters that are emphatically portrayed as altruists rather than egotists, one is a servant, namely, Paolo, who is not afraid to tell his master Leonardo the truth. The other altruist is old Fulgenzio, the friend of both families. His moralizing mentality that emphasizes reason recalls Ridolfo (*The Coffeehouse*). But Fulgenzio is more serene. In the end he has to resign himself to a passably acceptable solution for Leonardo. He can no longer change people and situations.

And finally Uncle Bernardino. A stark contrast to Fulgenzio, he is perhaps the only truly sardonic character Goldoni ever created. His manner of refusing to help Leonardo in any way whatsoever has great dramatic impact.·

The egocentricity of the young representatives of the middle class is basically derived from a lack of genuine relationships to persons and objects, which corresponds to a lack of authentic values or of values as such. The selfishness, however, of the only forcefully portrayed exponent of the old middle-class generation is derived from a petrified striving for purely material goods: the quintessence of avarice. Anyone who dares touch upon it becomes the target of masterful nastiness. What has become of Goldoni's habitual optimism?

The trilogy shows the man and artist Goldoni in his resigned goodbye to the principal character of his work, the Venetian middle class.

It is important that the three different styles of the three plays be amalgamated into an exciting, yet melancholy entity. It should bring together the colorful vitality of the dialogue in the first play, the psychologically intense atmosphere of the second play, and the return to the true proportions of sober reality in the third.

Since the beginning of the twentieth century Goldoni research has been suggesting that the trilogy be played in sequence, better yet, combined into a single play. (As was done by Giorgio Strehler in 1954.) This procedure permits the deletion of a few weak episodes (especially in *Summer-vacation Adventures* and in *The Return*). More than that, it stresses the lyricism that arises out of human beings caught in an extensive social crisis.

Much Ado in Chiozza

The original subject of this play seems to be the same as Shakespeare's *Much Ado about Nothing*. It is tempting to consider the comparisons one might make about the way in which each of the two poets handled this "nothing." We are again immediately faced with the problem of an adequate translation of the title of Goldoni's comedy, *Le baruffe chiozzotte*.

Baruffare means to quarrel, to wrangle, but the Venetian variant is less predominantly physical. It means settling an argument mainly with words and gestures. In this case, the cause of the disagreement is a slice of baked pumpkin, a real nothing that is completely forgotten at the end.

A fall morning in the little fishing town of Chiozza (the Chióggia of today), in the southern part of the Venetian lagoon. The men are still out at sea. They fish in cutters with yellow sails, each of which is distinguished by a colorful symbol.

But the morning is far from colorful. The sirocco is blowing in from the land, shrouding everything in a pale diffused light. The women are sitting in the street outside their houses, making lace, an old craft that is native to the islands of the lagoon and by which they try to supplement the meager earnings of the men. Naturally the talk is about marriage, a big problem, because of the forty thousand inhabitants a good thirty thousand are women.

The sea is their ever-present fate. The young women whom Goldoni places in the center of the action are not, according to conventional theater, daughters of the family. They are sisters and sisters-in-law. Winter is approaching. Hot baked slices of pumpkin are being sold, a cheap delicacy that helps pass the time.

The vendor's cry falls into the conversation of the women, who all know each other, who are always each other's friends and enemies during the long monotonous months of waiting for the men. Any change is welcome, even Toffolo, who is just making his appearance. He is one of the few men who stay behind, who are not able to go out fishing. He is the scorned bait fisherman, who peddles vegetables in a little boat along the coast.

He is a simpleton, but quite crafty. As he steps from woman to woman, the reactions of the women build as in an ascending arpeggio, from one lace-making pillow to the next. Thus the characterization of each starts. Meanwhile Toffolo does not notice that Lucietta has hooked him on her line. First she gets him to offer her slices of pumpkin, and then she uses him for her little scenes of jealousy. Until the biggest quarrel is in full swing . . . about nothing.

There is a temporary truce when the men come home. They are not supposed to find out about anything. But after a while (Pasqua: "If we women can't talk we burst") they, too, are dragged in. It hails insinuations, suspicions; a stone is thrown. The court

adjunct is asked to mediate. Even the engagement between Titta Nane and Lucietta breaks up.

At the end the waves flatten again as after any
storm, and as soon as the sky is definitely clear, three
marriages are celebrated. The dancing of the forlana
concludes the events of the day, and the court adjunct, Isidoro (alias Goldoni), steps aside and lets the
true protagonist, the fishing population, have the floor.

This play, which is about much ado about nothing,
is anything but a farce, and much more than a comedy
in the conventional sense. Certain situations are, of
course, comedy situations (when, for instance, one of
the women feigns deafness during the interrogation, or
the duet of invectives from window to window, etc.),
but there is not a single comic character, not even the
court clerk. His mechanical delivery of the official
texts only stresses the lifelessness of the law, of something abstract that these people do not understand and
therefore fear.

The fishing people live in a world of their own, as
illustrated by the nature of the characters. Each is so
completely integrated in the community that one or
the other may stand out according to the dramatic
requirements but is unthinkable isolated from the
others. For this reason an individual analysis of the
characters is difficult. It does not render the vital relationship of the individual to the community, or the
very special lyrical interplay between the two. With
this in mind, let us look at some of the characters.

Lucietta is the young woman most sharply in the
foreground. With female malice she promptly reacts,
from the first scene on, against little Checca, who had
the affrontery to hint at the homecoming of Lucietta's
fiancé, Titta Nane. This sets the avalanche in motion.
She is impulsive, vivacious, her stubbornness contains
a great deal of pride but also dignity. When she quar-

rels with her fiancé, she will not for anything in the world admit that she has feared for him for nights on end while he was out at sea. Love and stubbornness are constantly seesawing inside her, and one never wins out over the other, outside appearances notwithstanding. She is the strongest figure in the play, and the most outspoken representative of the people.

Titta Nane, too, is proud and stubborn, and in love. When he finds out that his fiancée, Lucietta, has spoken to another man, improper conduct in those days, he becomes very angry and breaks with her. They match each other in stubbornness, but he is awkward to boot and incapable of making amends when necessary. The last quarrel between them, before the final yes, is a splendid scene:

> LUCIETTA: You rotten scoundrel you!
> TITTA NANE: Shut your mouth!
> LUCIETTA: Are you going to drop me then?
> TITTA NANE: Are you going to do a thing like that to me again?
> LUCIETTA: No.
> TITTA NANE: Do you like me then?
> LUCIETTA: Yes.

And now Titta Nane makes his pledge that sounds like a taking of possession: "You are my wife!"

Checca is the youngest and a little underdeveloped for a girl of eighteen. She wants to get married for marriage's sake. Titta Nane is a fine-looking man, a respected fisherman. It would be wonderful if she could snatch him away from Lucietta, no matter by what means. It is hard to tell whether Checca is very naive or very crafty. In the end she contents herself with Toffolo, the bait fisherman. He does not even get a yes when he offers marriage—when her sister asks her if she wants him, she merely replies: "And why not?" Otherwise, she mainly thinks about the official dowry, which the court adjunct has promised her.

Vicenzo is called *paron* by the other fishermen, which means the owner of a fishing boat. But he does not go out fishing, and Goldoni does not tell us if he lost his boat at sea (where would he find the money to buy a new boat?), or if he suffered a physical disability during a mishap. At any rate, he has become a fish vendor. The other men would prefer to sell their catch exclusively to him because he is one of them, holds a position of authority to which all voluntarily submit, and does not cheat them, unlike the buyers from the city, "with their velvet caps" who "make money by the sweat of others." (Goldoni sharply criticized the middle class, from which he has by now completely turned away.)

Fortunato is a key figure in the play (often totally misunderstood). He, too, is a *paron*, a former owner of a fishing boat, and the oldest of the returning fishermen. Goldoni makes him swallow his syllables (he does *not* stammer), but the comic effect has its origin in the historical living conditions of these men. According to Manlio Dazzi, the *Complaint of the Venetian Fishermen*, 1570, which Goldoni did not know, used the same manner of speech. It may have been caused by the difficult communication in storm and wind when only shreds of sound are audible, or else by missing teeth. But, especially in characterization of such an old person, it indicates, according to B. Schacherl, not only "a stenography of the soul, but also a downright refusal to communicate, almost a return to primitive conditions, to unmitigated contact with the elements, the wind, the sea, the fish."

Of Fortunato, Schacherl wrote. "Humanity is a world of emotions, not of communication or expression. The others are still butting against the world with word inventions, insults, screams, and gestures, whereas he has become an integral part of the world."

He negates language, and when he does speak on occasion, it is only in thrifty words and images that reach the person at whom they are aimed.

The part of Isidoro has all too often been cast and directed carelessly. It must be properly understood in its threefold significance. First, we have Goldoni's memories of Chiozza that led to his understanding of the fishermen and his love for them. He had got to know the fishermen when he accompanied his father on visits to his patients, and later when he worked as a court adjunct at the local criminal court. (He was, at the time, living in the house of the Venetian woman painter Rosalba Carriera, which is far from being the only memory he uses in the play.)

The second significance of the part of the adjunct Isidoro is as a representative of administrative bureaucracy rather than of the jurisdiction that Venice exercised over the little town of Chiozza. It offers Isidoro alias Goldoni the opportunity to enter into the action merely as a mediating private citizen since the quarrel is legally irrelevant.

Hidden within this function is a slap at the bureaucratized "regime" of Venice: the big city and the vital as well as the autonomous world of the people of Chiozza are separated by more than a couple of hours ride through the lagoon.

The third function of the role of Isodoro is to allow (with his various attractive human weaknesses) dramatist Goldoni, in the guise of a mediating private person, to speak through Isodoro. He speaks in the disguise of an underpaid adjunct, with great discretion. Without a hint of paternalism, as might be tempting, he lets the people themselves find the main solution. As though this were not enough, he even allows the people to put him in his place: the forlana will be danced in the street, not in the manorhouse as he had suggested. Isidoro-Goldoni steps aside.

After Beolco's work, not many Italian plays used dialect on such a high artistic level. In *Much Ado in Chiozza* the dialect is in no way a limitation. It possesses the full width and psychological elasticity of a valid language and must be understood as such. (School Italian would have sounded stilted and foreign, too "literary" with its limited tradition.) The consciously created musical rhythm is striking. From the start it sets up the general atmosphere and each separate situation, including the musical choreographic groupings.

Goldoni's method, in which the style of the language indicates the style of the action and thereby the style of the performance, reaches a high point of perfection in this play. Choric structure and natural rhythm, from language to movement and back from movement to language, make up the essential artistic structure. The recognition of this structure is the basic prerequisite for an adequate translation. If the direction is not visibly motivated by the language, it is infallibly unpoetic, in other words a failure.

Another point: The speech of the inhabitants of Chiozza is slower than that of the Venetian city dwellers. (A foreigner who sees an Italian production of the play may not be aware of this and does not realize it automatically.) Consequently, the gestures are also slower and more economical.

Isidoro-Goldoni speaks city-Venetian dialect, of course. A subtle distinction that can hardly be rendered in translation. One should know that the distinction exists as an additional characterization of the two groups: Isidoro and the fishing population.

In *Much Ado in Chiozza* Goldoni offered the timeless autonomous world of simple people, after his sadly disappointed goodbye to the Venetian middle class (*Summer-vacation Trilogy*). It is the most modern of his plays. It would be idle to speculate how Goldoni's theater might have developed further if he had not been forced to move to France ("at my age one must live with one's enemies"). It is sufficiently significant that this particular play in this form stands as it were like a legacy at the end of Goldoni's development.

It can be said that Goldoni stood at the threshold of the world that was to become the world of the Sicilian writer Giovanni Verga, the founder of verismo, the father of neorealism. Without wishing to pursue this line in detail all the way to the present, we do wish to point to *The House by the Medlar Tree*. In this novel Verga drew an unforgettable picture of the world of the fishermen. This novel was the basis of the magnificent film *La terra trema*, which Luchino Visconti shot on location in Aci Trezza.

Aci Trezza and Chiozza may differ as to time, environment, mood, action, and the personal style of the two authors; Verga's fishermen may be Sicilian and Goldoni's Venetian, quite different in character and life style. Yet, their world is the same, self-contained, compact, a world that still exists to this day.

True, Verga placed the social and economic conditions of his time accusingly into the foreground making them painfully acute, and his love for these people was accompanied by bitter pessimism. Whereas Goldoni's love is coupled with hope, which is all the more surprising since he has ventured into a new stratum of society and is emphasizing a new social class that is in no way his own. We do not know if it was the frankness of these people, whose social status was barely above servants and just below peasants, their solidly self-contained world, that gave him this hopefulness.

The actual play of *Much Ado in Chiozza* is about the love story of Lucietta and Titta Nane, but the action is carried by the fishermen and their women as a group. The starkness of the social reality is almost veristic. (The words of welcome to the returning boat are sparing indeed.) This social reality permeates everything, although or especially because, allusion is made to it only indirectly, as though coincidentally. (Death at sea, the anguish at home, the exploitation by the merchants.) The allusions are made by people who are talking about something they take for granted. They see the conditions of their lives as a fixed invariable.

Research into the historical reality of eighteenth-century Chiozza gives a picture of the life of the fishermen who inspired Goldoni to write *Much Ado in Chiozza*. A hard life, because of the long absence at sea. The boats were too small, the work paid little, and the fatality rate was high.

The critic G. Lunardi wrote:

> And just because of this age-old habit of misery, danger, and deprivation, and in spite of the dramatic background, perhaps the purest, clearest laughter in our greatest literature of the theater arises from the events and the persons in *Much Ado in Chiozza*. One is the comedy born of ignoring reality, and the other is the laughter born of reality, no matter how dramatic the background. It is a testimony of conscious confidence in the human being rather than blind, prejudiced optimism.

On the basis of such an atmosphere, the play does not portray rebellion against fate, as Verga showed it. It does not lead to acts of violence. No knife is pulled in earnest, and the stone someone throws hits only by accident. During a brief scene, the women do attack each other bodily, a bit of stage business that heightens the effect of the preceding verbal exchange.

Two subjects then, the love story, and the social human world of the fishing people with its needs and its values. The total is held together by an unusual lyricism, derived from the musical rhythm of the words; the play is a score for voices, miming, and movement, in which all actors participate.

Unfortunately, *Much Ado in Chiozza* is insufficiently known abroad and has not been properly understood. A remarkable beginning was, however, made in the theater of the miners' town of Senftenberg in 1959–60 under the direction of Klaus Gendries.

A Piccolo Teatro di Milano production of *Much Ado in Chiozza*, directed by Giorgio Strehler, opened on 29 November 1964 at the Teatro Lirico in Milano.

After Simoni and Visconti, as well as after his various own productions that reactivated and intensified "Goldoni's conversation" with the audience (and in view of the many contributions of research work since the International Goldoni Congress in 1957), Strehler could assume that his countrymen were familiar with the social background of Goldoni's theater. Therefore, this production created less surprise in Italy than abroad (during the European tour of 1966), where people apparently still have difficulties accepting the fact of Goldoni's social consciousness. They are reluctant to get rid of the image of Goldoni, the good guy, and of the frame of "folklore" or "milieu" that goes along with the same tendency.

Goldoni, on the other hand, went further and further afield. In *Much Ado in Chiozza* the example of the fishing population led to his discovery of the world of the common people: with their uncomplicated feelings, their weaknesses and values, their dignity. And he trusted them.

Strehler knew from a critical evaluation of the text that content and form show a path that reaches all the way to the present. They show that path, but one can walk on it only to a certain extent. One cannot stride on it without losing the ground of the reality of Goldoni's time, "without going against the principles of true realism," as the Piccolo Teatro saw it.

It is precisely this new path, which is so interesting to Italian literature and to the history of theater, that has caught the particular attention of Strehler, who feels almost obliged to give the audience a sociological explanation for not making the message of the play more modern still.

In the foreword in the program of the Piccolo Teatro, Strehler wrote:

> If it is true that a great writer always reaches the point at which he gives to his work a stimulating reality-related content, with subjects and highlights that precede only recently outlined human and social possibilities, then it is also true that his anticipations must maintain a certain connection with the obvious, generally accepted reality, and not stray into an escape that would be no less sterile and hollow than the tired repetition of the subjects and forms of a dead past.

Like Visconti before him, Strehler developed the form and the special lyricism of his production on the basis of the directions given by Goldoni's dialogue. In his hands the dialogue sounds surprisingly modern, thanks to his extreme rigor, clarity, and relentless intellectual presence.

A modern expression for an old reality.

About this production the writer Alfonso Lazzari noted:

> *Much Ado in Chiozza* offers the stark, hard, manly and completely human picture of a social reality that stands outside of history, because it is the social reality of a subordinate class of simple people whose unending toil does not make his-

tory. In other words, a reality of the people that is authentic in its very eternalness. This is brought out in the direction by the gestures and interrelationships that have always been valid in the community of the fishing people and to which the actors lend expression. Strehler's direction follows an emphasized choric concept.

Goldoni's very own choric concept is the most clearly rendered reflection of a community that completely absorbs its members. It is admirable to what extent Strehler's direction expressed this aspect by sheer movement. By means of this movement Strehler also succeeded in showing the eternalness of the world of the fishing people. (The span of expression reaches in this case from an occasional echo of the antique chorus to the concentrated symbolism of our time.)

Since time immemorial, women have been alone with their anguish during the long months of waiting for the men at sea to return. The monotony gradually changes to a crescendo of expectation, as the time for the return draws nearer, and with it the renewal of life. The increasing expectation among the lace-making women is right at the outset one of Strehler's most successful compositions. (He uses the entire width of the stage for his mise en scène.) Then the emotions are added. Incidents of jealousy about the returning men, the exchange of epithets, follow so naturally as though they were a by-product of the reawakening of all the senses. Life in the community has always been subject to the seasons. Separation and reunion, work, death, and love, the elemental world of the fishing people, from which they derive their standards, their own laws.

Strehler's special direction of the movements, which are always related to the collective, produced a feeling of something "bigger" even in the spectator who was not familiar with Italian, of something standing above and beyond the emotions, no matter what may have triggered them.

Thus, the love story between Lucietta and Titta Nane is restored to the proportions that Goldoni intended. Because Goldoni did not build everything around this love story (which would have made it a love play). Instead he fitted the lovers into the community with its life cycles and its customs. The community is the sole and true carrier of the action.

The theater critic Siegfried Melchinger wrote:

> Just as Goldoni's advance toward realism was swept along by his knowledge of the people . . . the director's philosophical humor felt itself swept along by constant discoveries of new true traits in the twelve characters that line up on stage to play life.
>
> Gorki said that one need only assemble a few sharply and truthfully drawn characters, and drama immediately occurred by itself. (Chekhov, the greatest of all realists, did not proceed otherwise.)

The many individual traits are distinguished according to age and character, often by seemingly insignificant gestures; and yet they unmistakably have a common denominator. With one exception, however: Toffolo, the cowardly bait fisherman. It is he who throws the stone (like a bad boy), and who runs to the authorities, thus creating an event out of an incident.

How dusty the courtroom looks, compared to the world of the fishing people, how poor and lifeless. At first, Isidoro-Goldoni, the young man from the city, is alone in the room. It is not an easy part. The way in which he puts on the official wig, or stamps a paper, tells more than words. But Strehler gave the key to his function later, during two additional moments. The first, when Isidoro, now a mediating private citizen, meets Madonna Libera again. (The most important part in the mediation had, at any rate, been given to Paron Vicenzo, i.e., to the people themselves.) She had played deaf during the questioning shortly before, and now she can hear perfectly. Both laugh heartily about the incident.

The already delicious courtroom scene thus gains additional significance. Isidoro accepted the deafness, but the private citizen and dramatist Goldoni saw through it from the start, and Madonna Libera also always knew that he knew. (Of course this irony is in no way directed at the people. It is not paternalism, but subtle mockery, directed at the administration's remoteness from life, paired with a fine dose of self-mockery.)

And then the end: dramatist and citizen Goldoni steps aside to let the people have their way. He removes himself to the proscenium during the dancing of the forlana on stage.

Basic to Strehler's direction was the rhythm of the action, derived from the previously discussed special quality of the slow cadence of the Chiozza dialect. This can lead the theatergoer to a misunderstanding to which Goethe fell victim. On 10 October 1786, he saw the play. He made the mistake of seeing the temperament projected in this play as characteristic of the Mediterranean people. Italians do not feel it that way. One only has to take a look at Goldoni's city-Venetian *Campiello*, which is also musically constructed, and one immediately notices the difference in temperament.

The dialect of modern Chióggia poses a totally different problem, which Strehler was not able to solve completely either. In order to make this dialect—which Goldoni used as a valid language and which was understood as such throughout northern Italy—relatively accessible to modern Italians, Strehler suppressed much of its originality while at the same time caricaturing the drawn-out final vowels by making them overlong. It would, I think, have been preferable to avoid this compromise and to interpret the action for the Italian public, as had been done for foreign audiences, mainly with movement and gesture based on the word cadence.

Goldoni elaborated musically-rhythmically on the special speech cadence (still contained in modern Chióggia dialect), and it certainly is Strehler's most important merit to have fully recognized this fact in the form of the play, and to have taken it into account. Of this aspect Melchinger wrote: "I had to see the performance for the second time before I noticed that each scene was composed like a piece of music (and I was reminded of Stanislavski, whose pupils report that he proceeded in a similar fashion)."

The rhythm of this word score offers many additional possibilities for the harmonious emphasizing of small traits and characteristics, and offers moreover important assistance in maintaining the tone, or overall concept, at all times. In this way one can more easily tell that the quarrel of the men is not in deep earnest, in spite of a symbolically pulled knife. It is carried by the wave of emotions that runs high due to the homecoming, and it is the same with the women's exchange of invectives from window to window. Strehler outdid himself in the final composition, in which the duet travels from the second floor to the basement and to the street, and back, scaring a couple of children who are silently playing on the sidewalk.

Strehler's rhythm is remarkable for still another reason: by consciously incorporating the means of expression into this form, its inner law and poetic magnetism create an antiillusory effect (in an unexpected, yet successful manner), and Strehler's interpretation strengthens this aspect still more.

The set designer Luciano Damiani followed an identical direction. As Visconti-Tosi before him, he reduced costumes (especially as far as the colors were concerned; his colors are gray, brown, black, and white; only Isidoro's red coat stands out) and constructions to the essential, and created extensive light effects.

Of the sets Melchinger wrote:

> Never before have characters become so plastic on stage. The wooden slope (on which the wooden shoes of the fishermen and the wooden sandals of the women clatter and resound) has been taken back to the preillusionist ground plan, which permits set constructions only on the side and allows for perspective in the background.
>
> The ground plan has been divided into light zones; the actors rarely appear in full light, but even as silhouettes, they still have a plastic effect.
>
> The change of light and shadow gives a deeper warmth to the colors. In place of the background perspective stands the sky. In the lighting that was found after innumerable tryouts and with infinite sensitivity shines the ocean, glows the autumn, sways the *azzurro*. (Blue as the measure of effervescence, according to Benn.)

A highly poetic set that leads the new means of expression, at which Goldoni had hinted, even far beyond verismo, directly to the present, by means of the interplay of all elements that are effective on stage with an extremely disciplined active understanding of the artistic form. Constant intellectual presence (and meticulous rehearsing) resulted in an uninterrupted flow that seems self-evident and does not necessarily have to be identical with naturalness. Because inadvertently Strehler has strayed from the path of realism. (In spite of his realist point of departure, which the former Strehler would have tried to intensify by a second or even a third production.)

The process that is taking place on stage, and in the receptivity of the spectators, is again one of form. It is not the actual content that expresses the form, but the form that has taken control of a content. The content cannot, however, lie on the same modern level as Strehler's instrumentation (if one wishes to read additional meaning into the foreword of the program of the Piccolo Teatro). But the ingenious direction completely covers this lurking discrepancy, and as a result most theater critics concentrated on Strehler more than on Goldoni.

BIBLIOGRAPHY

1. Plays by Carlo Goldoni

The Addlepated Lady, or the Infatuated Widow—*La donna di testa debole, o sia La vedova infatuata.*

Aeneas in Latium—*Enea nel Lazio.*

The Antique Dealer's Family—*La famiglia dell'antiquario.*

Apathy—*L'apatista, o sia L'indifferente.*

Artemisia.

The Ball—*Il festino.*

The Bankruptcy, or the Failed Merchant—*La bancarotta, o sia Il mercante fallito.*

Beautiful Giorgiana—*La bella Giorgiana.*

Belisarius—*Belisario.*

Camilla's Tribulations—*Le inquietudini di Camilla.*

Campiello.

The Capricious Woman—*La donna stravagante.*

The Cavalier of Good Taste—*Il cavaliere di buon gusto.*

The Cheat, or Foppish Anthony—*Il frappatore, o Tonin Bella Grazia.*

The Clever Lady's Maid—*La cameriera brillante.*

The Coffeehouse—*La bottega del caffè.* Translated by Henry B. Fuller (New York: French, 1925).

The Contriving Woman—*La donna di moneggio.*

The Cunning Widow—*La vedova scaltra*. Translated as "The Artful Widow" by Frederick Davies, in *Four Comedies* (Baltimore: Penguin Books, 1968).

A Curious Accident—*Un curioso accidente*. Translated and adapted as *A Curious Mishap* by Richard D. T. Hollister (Ann Arbor, Mich.: Wahr, 1924). Based on the 1892 Helen Zimmern translation.

The Dalmatian—*La dalmatina*.

The Dancing School—*La scuola di ballo*.

The Discreet Wife—*La dama prudente*.

Domestic Bickerings—*I puntigli domestici*.

Don Juan Tenorio, or The Debauchee—*Don Giovanni Tenorio, o sia Il dissoluto*.

The Dutch Doctor—*Il medico olandese*.

The Eccentric Old Man—*Il vecchio bizzarro*.

The Eccentric Woman—*La donna bizzarra*.

The English Philosopher—*Il filosofo inglese*.

The Fair Savage—*La bella selvaggia*.

The Fan—*Il ventaglio*. Translated by E. and H. Farjeon, in *Three Comedies* (New York: Oxford University Press, 1961).

The Fanatic Poet—*Il poeta fanatico*.

The Father of a Family—*Il padre di famiglia*.

The Father through Love—*Il padre per amore*.

The Feigned Invalid—*La finta ammalata*.

The Feudatory—*Il feudatario*.

The Fickle Woman—*La donna volubile*.

The Flatterer—*L'adulatore*.

The Fond Mother—*La madre amorosa*.

The Funny Theater—*Il teatro comico*. Translated as *The Comic Theatre* by John W. Miller (Lincoln: University of Nebraska Press, 1969).

The Gambler—*Il giuocatore*.

The Gentleman and the Lady, or the Cicisbei—*Il cavaliere e la dama, o I cicisbei*.

Gentlemen of the Old School—*I rusteghi*. Translated as "The Boors" by I. M. Rawson, in *Three Comedies* (New York: Oxford University Press, 1961).

A Girl of Honor—*La putta onorata*. Translated as

"The Good Girl," in *Four Comedies* (London: Palmer, 1922).

The Good Compatriot—*Il buon compatriotto.*

The Good Family—*La buona famiglia.*

The Good Genius and the Bad Genius—*Il genio buono e il genio cattivo.*

The Good Mother—*La buona madre.*

The Good Wife—*La buona moglie.*

La Griselda.

The Harassed Millionaire—*Il ricco insidiato.*

Henry, King of Sicily—*Enrico, re di Sicilia.*

Hircana at Isfahan—*Ircana in Ispaan.*

Hircana in Julfa—*Ircana in Julfa.*

The Honorable Todero the Grouch—*Sior Todero brontolon.*

The Housekeeper—*La castalda.*

The House Party—*La villeggiatura.*

The Housewives—*Le massere.*

The Impostor—*Il raggiratore.*

The Impresario from Smirna—*L'impresario delle Smirne.* Translated, in *Four Comedies* (London: Palmer, 1922).

The Inquisitive Women—*Le donne curiose.*

The Intrepid Woman—*La donna forte.*

The Jealous Miser—*Il geloso avaro.*

The Jealous Women—*Le donne gelose.*

The Jealousy of Harlequin—*La gelosia di Arlecchino.*

Justin—*Giustino.*

A Lady of Charm—*La donna di garbo.*

The Liar—*Il bugiardo.* Translated by Grace Lovat Fraser (New York: Knopf, 1927).

The Lovers—*Gl'innamorati.*

The Loving Servant Maid—*La serva amorosa.*

The Loves of Alexander the Great—*Gli amori di Alessandro Magno.*

The Loves of Harlequin and Camilla—*Gli amori di Arlecchino e di Camilla.*

The Lucky Heiress—*L'erede fortunata.*

The Malcontents—*I malcontenti.*

A Man of the World—*L'uomo di mondo*. Also known as *Il momolo cortesan*.

Marriage by Competition—*Il matrimonio per concorso*.

The Merchants—*I mercanti*.

The Merry Cavalier—*Il cavaliere giocondo*.

Metempsychosis, or The Pythagorean Transmigration —*La metempsicosi, ossia La pitagorica trasmigrazione*.

The Military Lover—*L'amante militare*.

Mirandolina—*La locandiera*. Translated by Frederick Davies, in *Four Comedies* (Baltimore: Penguin Books, 1968). Also translated as *The Mistress of the Inn* by Merle Pierson (Madison, Wisc.: Dramatic Society, 1912); and as "Mine Hostess" by Clifford Bax, in *Three Comedies* (New York: Oxford University Press, 1961).

The Miser—*L'avaro*.

The Mishap, or The Imprudent Chatterer—*Il contrattempo, o sia Il chiacchierone imprudente*.

Molière—*Il Molière*.

Much Ado in Chiozza—*Le baruffe chiozzotte*. Translated as "The Squabbles of Chioggia" by Charles W. Lemmi in the periodical *The Drama* 15 (1914): 346–533.

The New House—*La casa nova*. Translated as "The Superior Residence" by Frederick Davies, in *Four Comedies* (Baltimore: Penguin Books, 1968).

The Obedient Daughter—*La figlia obbediente*.

One of the Last Nights of the Carnival—*Una delle delle ultime sere di Carnovale*.

Pamela Married—*Pamela maritata*.

Pamela the Spinster—*Pamela nubile*.

Paternal Love, or The Grateful Servant—*L'amore patterno, o sia La serva riconoscente*.

The Persian Bride—*La sposa persiana*.

The Peruvian Woman—*La peruviana*.

The Portrait of Harlequin—*Il ritratto d'Arlecchino*.

The Post Inn—*L'osteria della posta*. Translated by W. Chambers, in *The Drama: Its History, Literature, and Influence on Civilization*, edited by A. Bates, vol. 5 (London, 1903–1904).

The Prodigal—*Il prodigo*. Also known as *Momolo sulla Brenta*.

The Prudent Man—*L'uomo prudente*.

The Public Square—*Il campiello*.

The Respectable Adventurer—*L'avventuriere onorato*.

The Restless Men—*I morbinosi*.

The Restless Women—*Le morbinose*.

The Return from Summer Vacation—*Il ritorno dalla villeggiatura*.

Rinaldo di Montalbano.

Rosmonda.

The Scotch Girl—*La scozzese*.

The Self-Lover—*L'amante di sè medesimo*.

The Servant of Two Masters—*Il servitore di due padroni*. Translated by Edward J. Dent, in *The Classic Theatre*, edited by Eric Bentley, vol. 1 (Garden City, N.Y.: Doubleday, Anchor, 1958).

The Son of Harlequin Lost and Found Again—*Il figlio d'Arlecchino perduto e ritrovato*.

The Spendthrift Miser—*L'avare fastueux*.

The Spirit of Contradiction—*Lo spirito di contraddizione*.

Summer-vacation Adventures—*Le avventure della villeggiatura*.

Summer-vacation Mania—*Le smanie per la villeggiatura*.

The Swindler—*L'impostore*.

Terence—*Il Terenzio*.

Il Torquato Tasso.

The True Friend—*Il vero amico*.

The Tutor—*Il tutore*.

The Unknown Woman Persecuted—*L'incognita perseguitata*.

The Upper Servant—*La donna di governo*.

The Venetian Lawyer—*L'avvocato veneziano*.

The Venetian Twins—*I due gemelli veneziani*. Translated by Frederick Davies, in *Four Comedies* (Baltimore: Penguin Books, 1968).

The Vengeful Lady—*La donna vendicativa*.
The War—*La guerra*.
The Ward—*La pupilla*.
The Well-meaning Grouch—*Le bourru bienfaisant*. Translated as *The Beneficent Bear* by Barrett H. Clark (New York: French, 1915).
We Reap as We Sow—*Chi la fa l'aspetta*.
The Wise Bride—*La sposa sagace*.
The Wise Wife—*La moglie saggia*.
The Witty Cavalier—*Il cavaliere di spirito*.
The Witty Widow—*La vedova spiritosa*.
The Woman Alone—*La donna sola*.
Women Are Touchy—*Le femmine puntigliose*.
Women at Home—*Donne di casa soa*.
Women's Gossip—*I pettegolezzi delle donne*.
Zoroaster—*Zoroastro*.

2. Editions of Collected Works by Carlo Goldoni

Corrispondenza diplomatica, edited by Di Tucci, 1932.
Lettere, edited by Masi, 1880.
Mémoires pour servir à l'historie de sa vie et celle de son thèâtre, 3 vols., 1787. Edited by Guido Mazzoni, 1907. Translated by John Black, *Memoirs of Goldoni Written by Himself, Forming a Complete History of His Life and Writing*, 2 vols., London: Colburn, 1814. Reprint, with essay by William Dean Howells, Boston: Osgood, 1877. Reprint, with introduction by William Drake, New York: Knopf, 1926.
Opere complete, 37 vols., edited by Musatti, Maddalena, and Orolani, 1907–1943.
Opere teatrali, 44 vols., 1788–93.
Scelta di commedie, 2 vols., edited by Masi, 1897.
Tutti le opere, 8 vols., edited by G. Ortolani, 1935–48.

INDEX